# Math in Focus

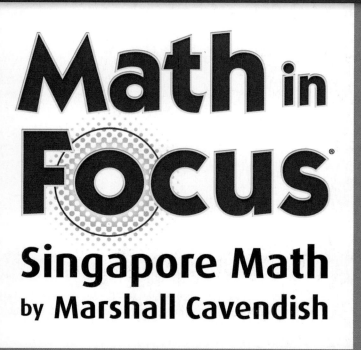

## Singapore Math
### by Marshall Cavendish

**Consultant and Author**
Dr. Fong Ho Kheong

**Authors**
Chelvi Ramakrishnan and Michelle Choo

**U.S. Consultants**
Dr. Richard Bisk
Andy Clark
Patsy F. Kanter

**Marshall Cavendish**
Education

US Distributor

HOUGHTON MIFFLIN HARCOURT

COMMON CORE

© 2013 Marshall Cavendish International (Singapore) Private Limited

**Published by Marshall Cavendish Education**
*An imprint of Marshall Cavendish International (Singapore) Private Limited*
Times Centre, 1 New Industrial Road, Singapore 536196
Customer Service Hotline: (65) 6411 0820
E-mail: tmesales@sg.marshallcavendish.com
Website: www.marshallcavendish.com/education

Distributed by
**Houghton Mifflin Harcourt**
222 Berkeley Street
Boston, MA 02116
Tel: 617-351-5000
Website: www.hmheducation.com/mathinfocus

First published 2013

Math in Focus® Grade 2 Student Book A
ISBN 978-0-547-87593-4

Printed in United States of America

2  3  4  5  6  7  8      1897      18  17  16  15  14  13
4500360944                        A  B  C  D  E

# Contents

## CHAPTER 1 Numbers to 1,000

Look for **Practice and Problem Solving**

| Student Book A and Student Book B | Workbook A and Workbook B |
| --- | --- |
| • **Let's Practice** in every lesson | • **Independent Practice** for every lesson |
| • Put on Your Thinking Cap! in every chapter | • Put on Your Thinking Cap! in every chapter |

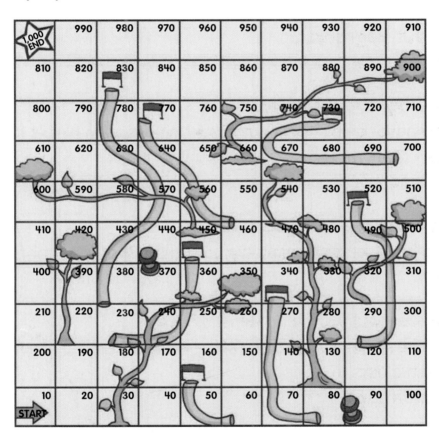

## Look for **Assessment Opportunities**

| Student Book A and Student Book B | Workbook A and Workbook B |
|---|---|
| • **Quick Check** at the beginning of every chapter to assess chapter readiness<br>• **Guided Practice** after every example or two to assess readiness to continue lesson | • **Chapter Review/Test** in every chapter to review or test chapter material<br>• **Cumulative Reviews** seven times during the year<br>• **Mid-Year and End-of-Year Reviews** to assess test readiness |

# CHAPTER
# 2 Addition up to 1,000

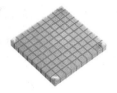

# Subtraction up to 1,000

# CHAPTER 4 Using Bar Models: Addition and Subtraction

# Multiplication and Division

# CHAPTER 6 Multiplication Tables of 2, 5, and 10

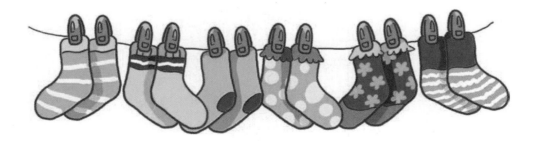

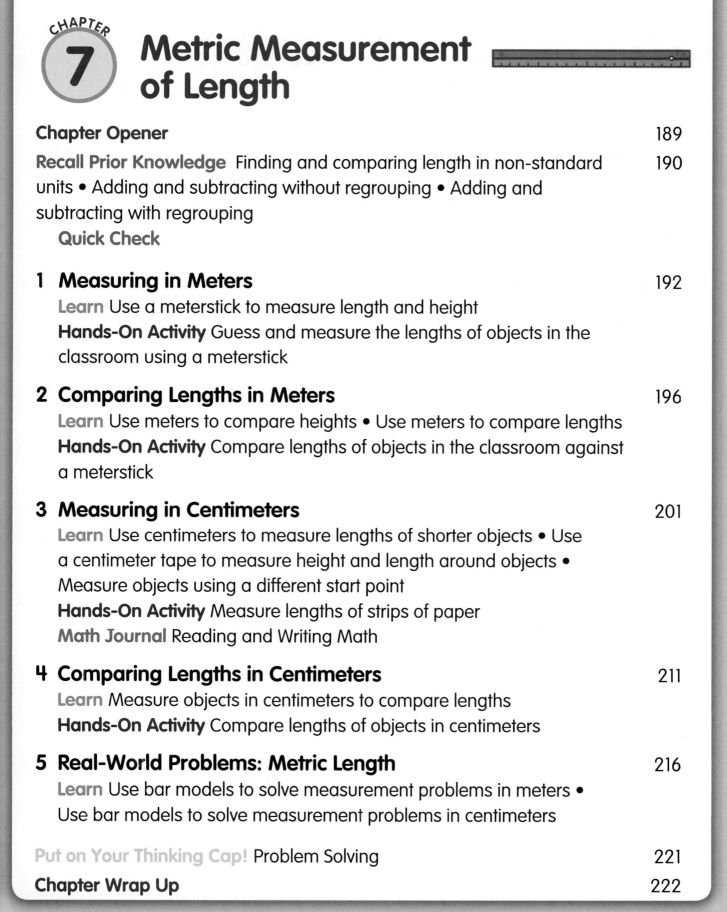

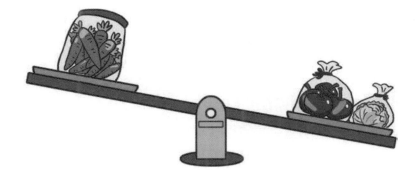

# CHAPTER
# 9 Volume

## Welcome to

# Math in Focus®

This exciting math program comes to you all the way from the country of Singapore. We are sure you will like all the different ways to learn math.

## What makes *Math in Focus*® different?

- **Two books** You don't write in the ▇ in this textbook. This book has a matching **Workbook.** When you see 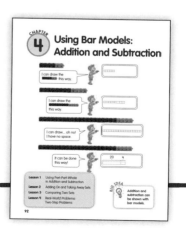 ON YOUR OWN you will write in the **Workbook.**

- **Longer lessons** Some lessons may last more than a day, so you can really understand the math.

- **Math will make sense** Learn to use number bonds to understand better how numbers work.

## In this book, look for

| Learn | Guided Practice | Let's Practice | ON YOUR OWN |
|---|---|---|---|
| This means you learn something new. | Your teacher helps you try some problems. | Practice. Make sure you really understand. | Now try some problems in your own **Workbook.** |

**Also look forward to** *Games, Hands-On Activities, Put on Your Thinking Cap!,* and more. Enjoy some real math challenges!

# What's in the Workbook?

*Math in Focus*® will give you time to learn important math ideas and do math problems. The **Workbook** will give you different types of practice.

- *Practice* problems will help you remember the new math idea you are learning. Watch for this 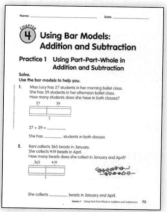 in your book. That will tell you which pages to use for practice.

- *Put on Your Thinking Cap!*

   *Challenging Practice* problems invite you to think in new ways to solve harder problems.

   *Problem Solving* gives you opportunities to solve questions in different ways.

- *Math Journal* activities ask you to think about thinking, and then write about that!

Students in Singapore have been using this kind of math program for many years. Now you can too — are you ready?

# 1 Numbers to 1,000

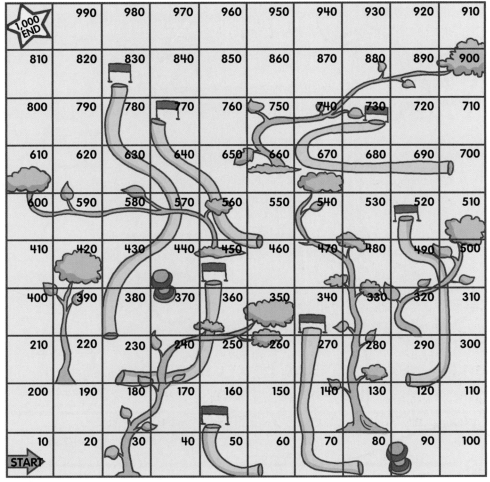

Move your counter up to the top of a tree when you land on its base.

Move your counter to the bottom of a pipe when you land at its top.

The first player to reach 1,000 wins the game!

Players: 2-4
You need:
- one counter for each player
- a number cube

BIG IDEA

Count and compare numbers to 1,000.

1

# Recall Prior Knowledge

## Number bonds

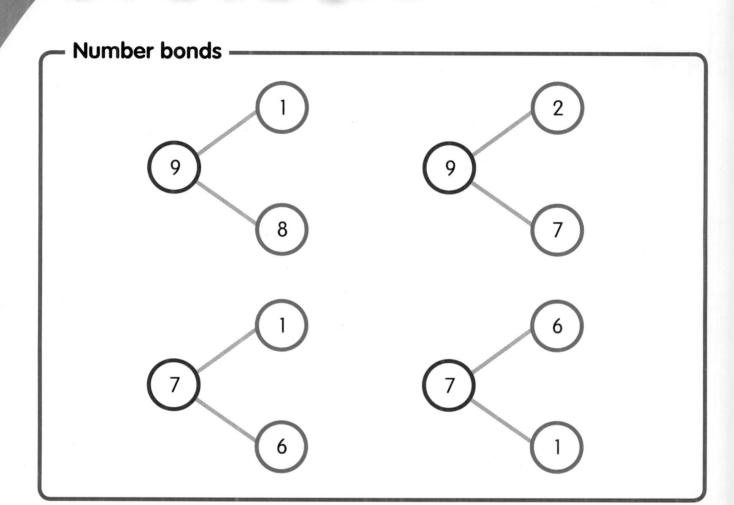

## Counting

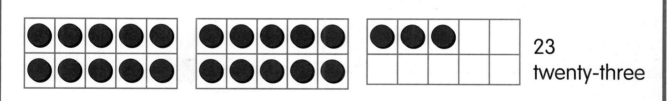

23
twenty-three

## Counting on from a given number

**1** **59**, 60, 61, 62, 63       **2** **96**, 97, 98, 99, 100

## Using objects to show numbers

63
sixty-three

## Using base-ten blocks to show numbers and place value

| Tens | Ones |
|:---:|:---:|
| 5 | 4 |

54

5 tens 4 ones make 54.
50 and 4 make 54.
54 is 50 and 4.
$50 + 4 = 54$

## Comparing numbers

**1** Compare 50 and 34.
5 tens is greater than 3 tens.
50 is greater than 34.

| Tens | Ones |
|:---:|:---:|
| 5 | 0 |
| 3 | 4 |

**2** Compare 82, 85, and 88.
The tens are equal.
2 ones is less than 5 ones.
5 ones is less than 8 ones.
The greatest number is 88.
The least number is 82.

| Tens | Ones |
|:---:|:---:|
| 8 | 2 |
| 8 | 5 |
| 8 | 8 |

## Making number patterns

**1**   48, 49, 50, 51, 52, 53, 54

**2**   73, 72, 71, 70, 69, 68, 67, 66

**3**   56, 58, 60, 62, 64, 66, 68, 70

## ✔ Quick Check

**Find the missing numbers.**

**1**   Show two ways of making 8.

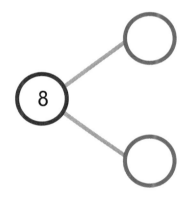

**What is the number shown by each model?**
**What is the number in words?**

**2**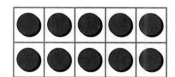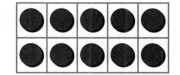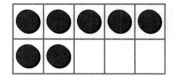

## What is the number shown by each model?
## What is the number in words?

| Tens | Ones |
|------|------|

**4**

## Find the missing numbers.

**5**  40 and ⬚ make 48.

**6**  56 is ⬚ and 6.

**7**  ⬚ + 9 = 79

## Answer True or False.

**8**  29 is greater than 43.

**9**  69 is less than 96.

**10**  87 is greater than 8 tens.

## Complete the number patterns.

**11**  22, 23, 24, ⬚, 26, ⬚

**12**  100, 95, 90, ⬚, ⬚, 75

# Counting

**LESSON 1**

## Lesson Objectives

- Use base-ten blocks to recognize, read, and write numbers to 1,000.
- Count on by 1s, 10s, and 100s to 1,000.

**You can use base-ten blocks to show numbers.**

Put 10 ⬛ together to make ▭.

Put together 10 ▭.

10 tens = 100

> 10, 20, 30, 40, 50, 60, 70, 80, 90, 100.
> One **hundred** !

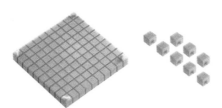

100     one hundred

108     one hundred eight

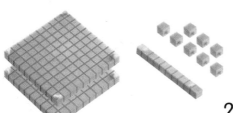

218     two hundred eighteen

# Guided Practice

## Find the missing numbers.

**1** How many 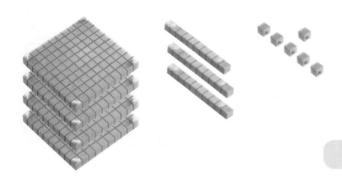 are there?

[   ] hundred [   ]

**2** How many ● are there?

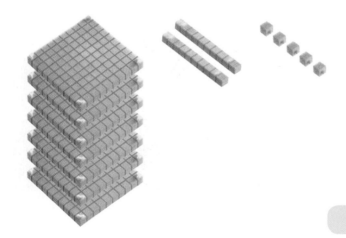

[   ] hundred [   ]

**3**

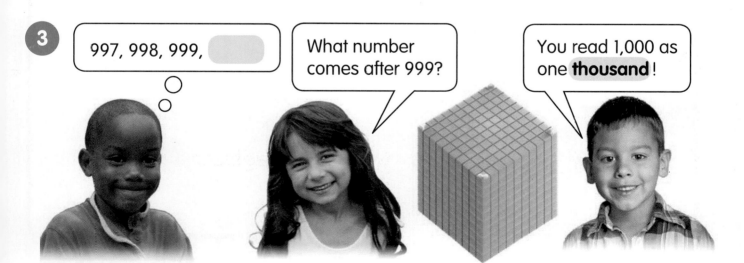

997, 998, 999, [   ]

What number comes after 999?

You read 1,000 as one **thousand**!

**Learn** You can use base-ten blocks to count on by ones.

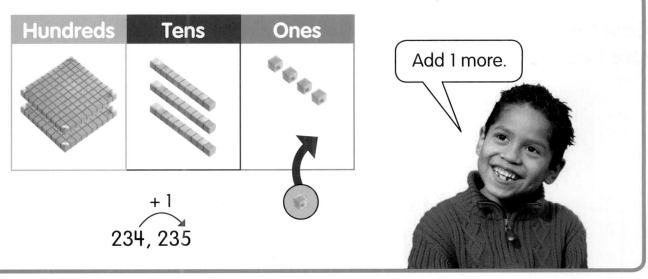

Add 1 more.

$+1$

234, 235

## Guided Practice

**Count on by ones.**
**Use base-ten blocks to help you.**

4   424, 425, 426, ____, ____, ____, ____, ____

**Learn** You can use base-ten blocks to count on by tens.

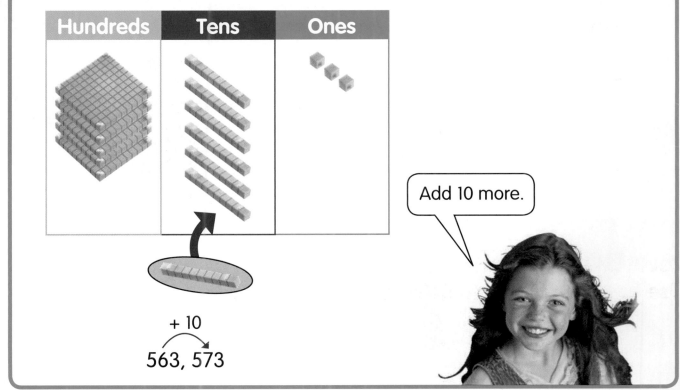

Add 10 more.

$+10$

563, 573

## Guided Practice

**Count on by tens.**
**Use base-ten blocks to help you.**

**5**  519, 529, 539, 549, ____, ____, ____, ____

**6**  740, 750, 760, 770, ____, ____, ____, ____

**Learn** **You can use base-ten blocks to count on by** **hundreds**.

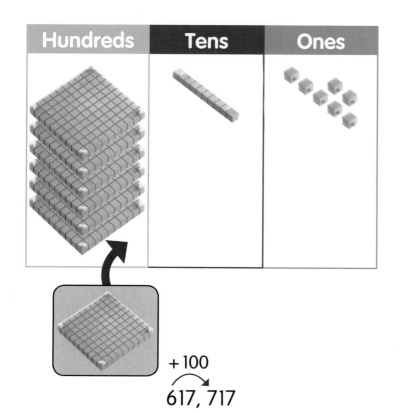

| Hundreds | Tens | Ones |
|---|---|---|

+ 100

617, 717

Add 100 more.

## Guided Practice

**Count on by hundreds.**
**Use base-ten blocks to help you.**

**7**  260, 360, 460, ____, ____, ____

**8**  435, 535, 635, ____, ____, ____

# Let's Practice

**What are the numbers shown by the base-ten blocks?**

**1**

| Hundreds | Tens | Ones |
|---|---|---|

**2**

| Hundreds | Tens | Ones |
|---|---|---|

**Count on.**
**Use base-ten blocks to help you.**

**3**   615, 616, 617, _____ , _____ , _____ , _____

**4**   468, 478, 488, _____ , _____ , _____ , _____

**5**   204, 304, 404, _____ , _____ , _____ , _____

ON YOUR OWN

Go to Workbook A:
Practice 1, pages 1–6

# 2 Place Value

## Lesson Objectives

- Use base-ten blocks and a place-value chart to read, write, and represent numbers to 1,000.

- Read and write numbers to 1,000 in standard form, expanded form, and word form.

**Vocabulary**
standard form
word form
expanded form

**Learn** **You can use base-ten blocks and a place-value chart to show a number.**

How many ▣ are there?

| Hundreds | Tens | Ones |
|----------|------|------|
| | | |
| 2 | 5 | 8 |

stands for
**2 hundreds**
or 200

stands for
**5 tens**
or 50

stands for
**8 ones**
or 8

2 0 0
5 0
8 ➡ 2 5 8

The digit 2 is in the hundreds place.

The digit 5 is in the tens place.

The digit 8 is in the ones place.

**Learn** **You can write numbers in word form, standard form, and expanded form.**

200, 50, and 8 make 258.

258 is the **standard form** of 258.

Two hundred fifty-eight is the **word form** of 258.

258 = 2 hundreds 5 tens 8 ones
     = 200 + 50 + 8

200 + 50 + 8 is the **expanded form** of 258.

## Guided Practice

**Fill in the missing numbers or words.**

1

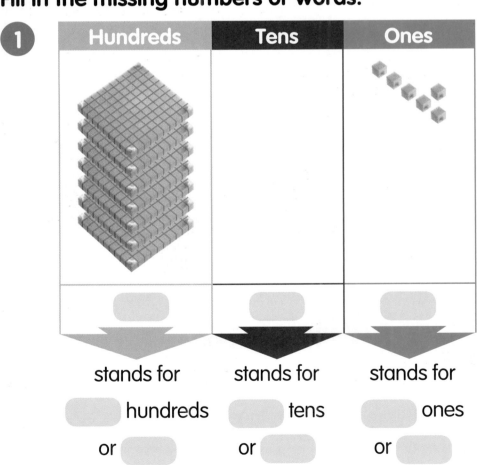

| Hundreds | Tens | Ones |
|---|---|---|

stands for    stands for    stands for

☐ hundreds  ☐ tens  ☐ ones

or ☐    or ☐    or ☐

**2** In 706,

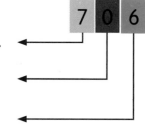

   **a**   the digit ⬚ is in the hundreds place.

   **b**   the digit ⬚ is in the tens place.

   **c**   the digit ⬚ is in the ones place.

**3** 700 and 6 make ⬚ .

**4** 706 is the ⬚ form of 706.

**5** Seven hundred six is the ⬚ form of 706.

**6** 706 = 7 hundreds ⬚ tens 6 ones

      = 700 + 6

   700 + 6 is the ⬚ form of 706.

> Do not add the tens because there are no tens.

**Find the missing numbers.**

**7**

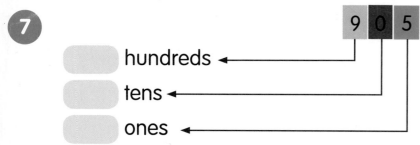

⬚ hundreds

⬚ tens

⬚ ones

**8** The word form of 905 is ⬚ .

# What are the numbers in word form?

**9** 256

**10** 380

**11** 471

**12** 762

# What are the numbers in standard form?

**13** Six hundred fifty

**14** 800 + 5

**15** 5 hundreds 3 tens

**16** 900 + 40 + 5

# What are the numbers in expanded form?

**17** 562

**18** 803

**19** 940

**20** 139

# Show the Number!

Players: 2
You need:
• base-ten blocks
• place-value charts

Player 1 shows Player 2 some base-ten blocks.

Player 2 counts the blocks and writes the number in the place-value chart. Player 2 then writes the number in standard form, word form, and expanded form.

Player 1 checks Player 2's answers.

Correct!

Take turns showing the base-ten blocks. Players get 1 point for every correct answer.

The player who gets more points wins!

# Let's Practice

**What are the numbers in standard form?**

**1** nine hundred twenty-three ⬚

**2** three hundred ten ⬚

**What are the numbers in word form?**

**3** 435 ⬚

**4** 960 ⬚

**Find the missing numbers.**

**5**

| Hundreds | Tens | Ones |
|----------|------|------|
| 3 | 4 | 6 |

stands for ⬚ hundreds or ⬚

stands for ⬚ tens or ⬚

stands for ⬚ ones or ⬚

**6**

| Hundreds | Tens | Ones |
|----------|------|------|
| 6 | 0 | 5 |

stands for ⬚ hundreds or ⬚

stands for ⬚ tens or ⬚

stands for ⬚ ones or ⬚

# Write the numbers in standard form, word form, and expanded form.

**7**

| Hundreds | Tens | Ones |
|---|---|---|

( ) ( ) ( )

**8**

| Hundreds | Tens | Ones |
|---|---|---|

( ) ( ) ( )

# Find the missing numbers or words.

**9** In the number 980,

**a** the digit 9 is in the _____ place,

**b** the digit 8 is in the _____ place, and

**c** the digit _____ is in the ones place.

ON YOUR OWN

Go to Workbook A:
Practice 2, pages 7–12

# LESSON 3 Comparing Numbers

**Lesson Objectives**

- Use base-ten blocks to compare numbers.
- Compare numbers using the terms **greater than** and **less than**.
- Compare numbers using symbols > and <.

**Learn** **You can use base-ten blocks to compare numbers.**

Which is greater, 235 or 146?

| | Hundreds | Tens | Ones |
|---|---|---|---|
| 235 | | | |
| 146 | | | |

Compare the hundreds.
2 hundreds is greater than 1 hundred.

235 is greater than 146.

You can write 235 > 146.

The symbol > stands for **greater than**.

Two numbers can have the same number of hundreds.
Then you compare the tens.

Which is less, 372 or 345?

| Hundreds | Tens | Ones |
| --- | --- | --- |
| 372 | | |
| 345 | | |

First, compare the hundreds.
They are the same.
Then, compare the tens.
4 tens is less than 7 tens.

345 is less than 372.

You can write 345 < 372.

The symbol < stands for **less than**.

Continued on next page

Compare 418 and 415.

Which is greater?

Which is less?

Two numbers can have the same number of hundreds and tens.
Then you compare the ones.

| | Hundreds | Tens | Ones |
|---|---|---|---|
| 418 | | | |
| 415 | | | |

First, compare the hundreds.
Both are the same.

Next, compare the tens.
Both are the same.

Then, compare the ones.
5 ones is less than 8 ones.

418 is greater than 415.

418 > 415.

415 is less than 418.

415 < 418.

# Guided Practice

**Answer with greater than or less than.**

 **1**

 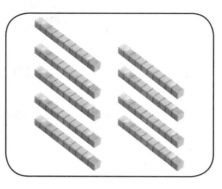

300 is  90.

**2**

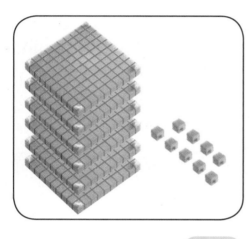 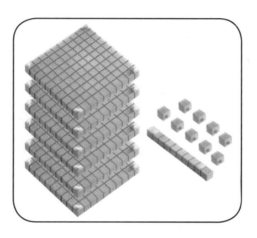

609 is _____ 619.

**Use base-ten blocks to compare the numbers.**
**Answer with greater than or less than.**

**3** 233 is _____ 333.

**4** 715 is _____ 709.

**5** 564 is _____ 560.

**6** 479 is _____ 497.

**Answer with > or <.**

**7** 578 ⬤ 478

**8** 826 ⬤ 890

**9** 495 ⬤ 490

**10** 879 ⬤ 897

# Roll and Show!

Players: 3
You need:
- a ten-sided die
- a sheet of paper

**STEP 1** Player 1 rolls the die three times to make a three-digit number.
Player 3 writes the number.

**STEP 2** Player 2 rolls the die three times to make another three-digit number.
Player 3 writes this number too.

**STEP 3** Player 3 looks at the numbers and writes **less than** or **greater than** between them.
The other players check the answer.

500 is greater than 300.
So, 547 is greater than 399.

**STEP 4** Take turns to roll and write!

The player with the most correct answers wins!

# Let's Practice

Use base-ten blocks to compare.
Answer with greater than or less than.

**1**

 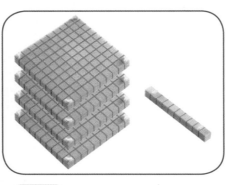

400 is [____] 410.

**2** 783 is [____] 837.    **3** 578 is [____] 944.

**4** 217 is [____] 158.    **5** 751 is [____] 570.

**6** 326 is [____] 234.

Use base-ten blocks to compare.
Answer with > or <.

**7**

 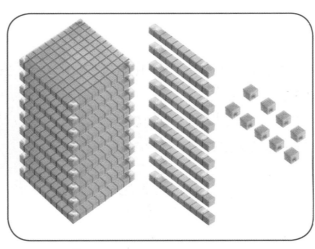

1,000 ⬤ 999

**8** 218 ⬤ 238    **9** 745 ⬤ 754

**10** 366 ⬤ 361    **11** 111 ⬤ 112

ON YOUR OWN

Go to Workbook A:
Practice 3, pages 13–14

# 4 Order and Pattern

**Lesson Objectives**

- Order three-digit numbers.
- Identify the greatest number and the least number.
- Identify number patterns.

**Learn** **You can use place-value charts to order numbers.**

Order 489, 236, and 701 from least to greatest.

| | Hundreds | Tens | Ones |
|---|---|---|---|
| 489 | 4 | 8 | 9 |
| 236 | 2 | 3 | 6 |
| 701 | 7 | 0 | 1 |

Compare the hundreds. 701 is greater than 489. 701 is greater than 236.

701 is the **greatest**.

236 is the **least**.

From least to greatest, the numbers are:

236 , 489 , 701
least

489 is greater than 236.

# Guided Practice

**Find the missing numbers.**

**1** Identify the greatest and least number.
Then, order 459, 574, and 558 from greatest to least.

| | Hundreds | Tens | Ones |
|---|---|---|---|
| 459 | 4 | 5 | 9 |
| 574 | 5 | 7 | 4 |
| 558 | 5 | 5 | 8 |

[____] is the greatest.

[____] is the least.

[____] , [____] , [____]
greatest

**Order the numbers from least to greatest.
Use a place-value chart to help you.**

**2** 707,  904,  762,  555

[____] , [____] , [____] , [____]
least

**READING AND WRITING MATH**
# Math Journal

**Choose the method you would use to compare the numbers.**

**1**  [ 247 ]   [ 724 ]   [ 274 ]   [ 427 ]

**a** I compare the ones first, next the tens and the hundreds last.

**b** I compare the tens first, next the hundreds and the ones last.

**c** I compare the hundreds first, next the tens and the ones last.

**d** I compare the hundreds first, next the ones and the tens last.

**2** Are the numbers ordered from greatest to least?
Explain why or why not.
Use a place-value chart to help you.

724    247    274    427

---

<sup>Learn</sup> **You can use a number line to find the missing number in a pattern.**

Find the missing numbers.

1 more than
253 is 254.

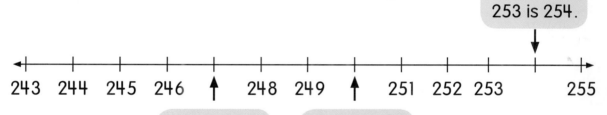

243  244  245  246  ↑  248  249  ↑  251  252  253      255

1 **more than**
246 is 247.

1 **less than**
251 is 250.

The rule for finding
the next number is
to add 1.

The missing numbers are 247, 250, and 254.

# Find the missing numbers.

**3**

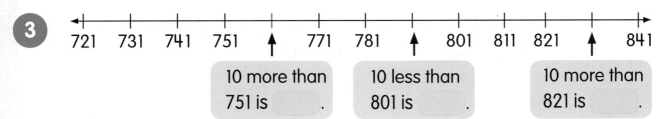

| 10 more than 751 is ____. | 10 less than 801 is ____. | 10 more than 821 is ____. |

**4**

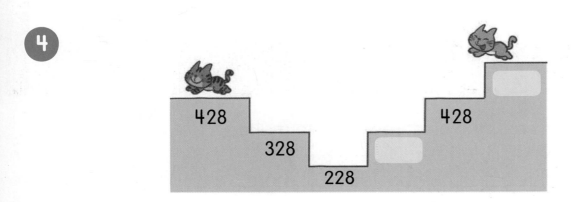

428   328   228   428

# Find the missing numbers.
## Use a place-value chart or number line to help you.

**5**   1 less than 999 is ____.

**6**   20 more than 415 is ____.

**7**   100 more than 900 is ____.

**8**   200 less than 635 is ____.

**9**   442, 542, 642, 742, ____, ____

**10**   298, 299, ____, ____, 302, 303

**11**   ____, 810, 820, ____, ____, 850

**12**   ____, ____, 332, 232, 132, ____

# Roll and Count!

Players: 6
You need:
- one ten-sided die
- one chart

**STEP 1** Player 1 rolls the die three times to make a three-digit number.
If the three-digit number is 900 or more, roll the die three more times to get a new number.

**STEP 2** Take turns rolling the die until every player has a three-digit number.

| Number | |
|---|---|
| 1 more than the number | |
| 1 less than the number | |
| 10 more than the number | |
| 10 less than the number | |
| 100 more than the number | |
| 100 less than the number | |

**STEP 3** Each player fills in a chart.

The player with all correct answers in the shortest time wins!

# Let's Explore!

Jesse and Cathy try to find out how many numbers there are from:

**1** 3 to 9        **2** 8 to 15        **3** 17 to 27

They use different ways to find the answer.

I count the numbers.
There are 7 numbers from 3 to 9.

Jesse

I subtract the numbers.
9 minus 3 is equal to 6.

Cathy

|  | | Jesse's Way | Cathy's Way |
|---|---|---|---|
| **1** | 3 to 9 | 7 | $9 - 3 = 6$ |
| **2** | 8 to 15 | 8 | $15 - 8 = 7$ |
| **3** | 17 to 27 | 11 | $27 - 17 = 10$ |

Raul

Raul checked the answers and showed that Jesse's way
was correct.
Then he looked at Cathy's and Jesse's answers and saw a pattern.
Jesse's answer was always 1 more than Cathy's answer.

Continued on next page

**Use what you have learned to answer each question.**

How many numbers are there from:

**4** 22 to 38?          **5** 44 to 79?          **6** 24 to 94?

**7** Check your answers to **4**, **5**, and **6** by counting.

## Let's Practice

**Order the numbers.**
**Use a place-value chart to help you.**

**1** Order the numbers from least to greatest.

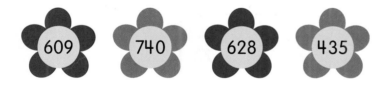

609    740    628    435

[    ] , [    ] , [    ] , [    ]
least

**2** Order the numbers from greatest to least.

368    555    357    699    553

[    ] , [    ] , [    ] , [    ] , [    ]
greatest

**Find the missing numbers.**
**Use a place-value chart or number line to help you.**

**3** 1 more than 293 is ____ .  **4** 10 more than 528 is ____ .

**5** 100 more than 190 is ____ .  **6** 20 more than 425 is ____ .

**7** 100 more than 762 is ____ .  **8** 200 more than 204 is ____ .

**Find the missing numbers.**
**Use a place-value chart or number line to help you.**

**9** 1 less than 717 is ____ .  **10** 5 less than 685 is ____ .

**11** 10 less than 480 is ____ .  **12** 30 less than 257 is ____ .

**13** 100 less than 921 is ____ .  **14** 200 less than 635 is ____ .

**Complete the number patterns.**
**Use place-value charts or number lines if you need to.**

**15** 203, ____ , 205, 206, 207, ____ , 209, ____ , ____

**16** 648, 658, ____ , 678, ____ , ____ , ____ , ____

**17** 721, 621, ____ , ____ , 321, ____ , ____ , ____

**18** 342, ____ , ____ , ____ , 338, 337, 336

ON YOUR OWN

Go to Workbook A:
Practice 4, pages 15–18

**PROBLEM SOLVING**

## Find the missing numbers.
## Use place-value charts or number lines to help you.

1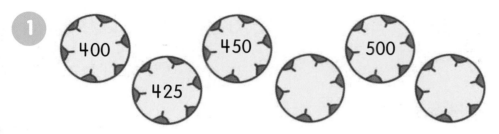

400   425   450   500

2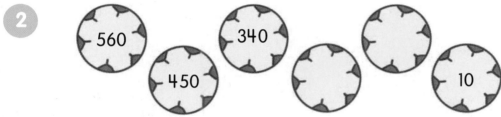

560   450   340   10

## Complete the number pattern.
Squeaky Squirrel is storing nuts for winter.
He adds 3 nuts each day for five days.
At the end of the fifth day, he has 50 nuts.

3 How many nuts did he have at the end of the first day?

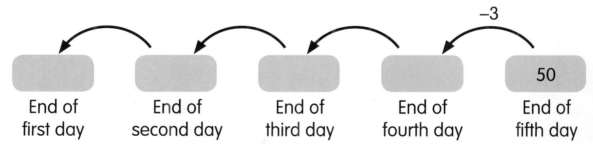

−3

| | | | | 50 |

End of first day | End of second day | End of third day | End of fourth day | End of fifth day

4 If Squeaky Squirrel continues to add 3 nuts every day, how many more days does he need to have 62 nuts?

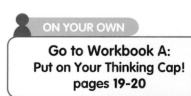

ON YOUR OWN

**Go to Workbook A:
Put on Your Thinking Cap!
pages 19-20**

# Chapter Wrap Up

You have learned...

 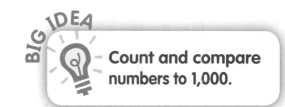

## Numbers to 1,000

### Read, Write, and Count
### Place Value
### Compare
### Order and Make Patterns

| Hundreds | Tens | Ones |
|---|---|---|
| | | |
| 3 | 4 | 6 |

stands for 3 hundreds or 300

stands for 4 tens or 40

stands for 6 ones or 6

**1** Order 976, 769, and 796 from greatest to least:

976 , 796 , 769
greatest

**2** Make patterns
- 205, 206, 207, 208
- 548, 558, 568, 578
- 834, 734, 634, 534

Standard form:
346

Word form:
three hundred forty-six

Expanded form:
300 + 40 + 6

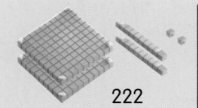 222

 235

222 is less than 235.
222 < 235
235 is greater than 222.
235 > 222

ON YOUR OWN

**Go to Workbook A: Chapter Review/Test, pages 21–24**

# CHAPTER
# 2 Addition up to 1,000

Mighty oaks from little acorns grow.
100, 200, 300, 400, 500, 600, 700, 800, 900, 1,000.
Out of a thousand acorns, only 1 might grow.
So find an acorn, plant it with love.
Watch it grow into the sky above.

BIG IDEA

Three-digit numbers can be added with and without regrouping.

# Recall Prior Knowledge

## Fact family

$2 + 3 = 5$        $3 + 2 = 5$        $5 - 2 = 3$        $5 - 3 = 2$

8 cubes

3 + 5

8 cubes

5 + 3

$3 + 5 = 5 + 3$

## Adding zero

$3 + 0 = 3$                    $0 + 99 = 99$

## Adding without regrouping

$62 + 5 = ?$

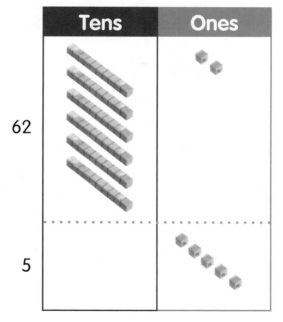

| Tens | Ones |
|------|------|
| 62 | 5 |

**Step 1**
Add the ones.

```
  Tens  Ones
    6    2
+        5
_____
         7
```

**Step 2**
Add the tens.

```
  Tens  Ones
    6    2
+        5
_____
    6    7
```

So, $62 + 5 = 67$.

## Adding with regrouping

57 + 5 = ?

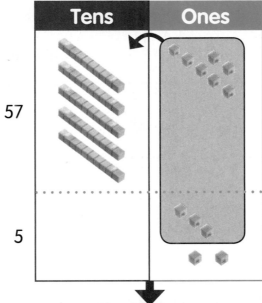

**Step 1**
Add the ones.

| Tens | Ones |
|------|------|
| ¹    |      |
| 5    | 7    |
| +    | 5    |
|      | 2    |

Regroup the ones.
12 ones = 1 ten 2 ones

**Step 2**
Add the tens.

| Tens | Ones |
|------|------|
| ¹    |      |
| 5    | 7    |
| +    | 5    |
| 6    | 2    |

So, 57 + 5 = 62.

## Adding three numbers

3 + 1 + 6 = ?

**Method 1**
3 + 1 + 6
4 + 6 = 10

**Method 2**
3 + 1 + 6
3 + 7 = 10

## Adding to solve real-world problems

Max sees 8 big birds.

There are 12 little birds too!

How many birds does Max see in all?

$8 + 12 = 20$

Max sees 20 birds altogether.

$$\begin{array}{r} {}^{1}\phantom{0} \\ 1\ 2 \\ +\ \ \ \ 8 \\ \hline 2\ 0 \end{array}$$

## ✔ Quick Check

**Which number sentences are in the same fact family as 7 + 6 = 13?**

**1**

| | | |
|---|---|---|
| $6 + 7 = 13$ | $7 - 6 = 1$ | $13 + 7 = 20$ |
| $13 - 7 = 6$ | $13 - 6 = 7$ | $7 + 13 = 20$ |

**Add.**

**2** $67 + 0 = $ 

**3** $0 + 43 = $ 

**4** $6 + 7 + 8 = $ 

**5** $5 + 6 + 4 = $ 

**6**
$$\begin{array}{r} 3\ 2 \\ +\ 5\ 7 \\ \hline \end{array}$$

**7**
$$\begin{array}{r} 7\ 8 \\ +\ 1\ 7 \\ \hline \end{array}$$

**Solve.**

**8** Hannah rode 12 miles on her bicycle on Monday.
On Tuesday, she rode another 17 miles.
How many miles did she ride in all?

# ① Addition Without Regrouping

## Lesson Objectives

- Use base-ten blocks to add numbers without regrouping.
- Add up to three-digit numbers without regrouping.
- Solve real-world addition problems.

**Vocabulary**
add
place-value chart

**Learn** **You can add using base-ten blocks and a place-value chart.**

163 + 5 = ?

| Hundreds | Tens | Ones |
|---|---|---|
| 163 | | |
| 5 | | |

**Step 1**
Add the ones.

$$\begin{array}{r} 1\ \ 6\ \ 3 \\ +\ \ \ \ \ \ 5 \\ \hline 8 \end{array}$$

3 ones + 5 ones = 8 ones

**Step 2**
Add the tens.

$$\begin{array}{r} 1\ \ 6\ \ 3 \\ +\ \ \ \ \ \ 5 \\ \hline 6\ \ 8 \end{array}$$

6 tens + 0 tens = 6 tens

**Step 3**
Add the hundreds.

$$\begin{array}{r} 1\ \ 6\ \ 3 \\ +\ \ \ \ \ \ 5 \\ \hline 1\ \ 6\ \ 8 \end{array}$$

1 hundred + 0 hundreds
= 1 hundred

So, 163 + 5 = 168.

## Learn You can add using base-ten blocks and a place-value chart.

271 + 27 = ?

| Hundreds | Tens | Ones |
|---|---|---|
| 271 | | |
| 27 | | |

**Step 1**
Add the ones.

```
  2 7 1
+   2 7
───────
      8
```

1 one + 7 ones = 8 ones

**Step 2**
Add the tens.

```
  2 7 1
+   2 7
───────
    9 8
```

7 tens + 2 tens = 9 tens

**Step 3**
Add the hundreds.

```
  2 7 1
+   2 7
───────
  2 9 8
```

2 hundreds + 0 hundreds = 2 hundreds

So, 271 + 27 = 298.

## Guided Practice

**Add.**

1  153 + 4 =

2  181 + 6 =

3  372 + 25 =

4  706 + 83 =

**Learn** **You can add using base-ten blocks and a place-value chart.**

145 + 352 = ?

| Hundreds | Tens | Ones |
|---|---|---|
| 145  | | |
| 352 | | |

**Step 1**
Add the ones.

```
  1 4 5
+ 3 5 2
─────────
      7
```

5 ones + 2 ones = 7 ones

**Step 2**
Add the tens.

```
  1 4 5
+ 3 5 2
─────────
    9 7
```

4 tens + 5 tens = 9 tens

**Step 3**
Add the hundreds.

```
  1 4 5
+ 3 5 2
─────────
  4 9 7
```

1 hundred + 3 hundreds
= 4 hundreds

So, 145 + 352 = 497.

## Guided Practice

**Find the missing numbers.**

**5**  623 + 254 = ?
Add the ones.
3 ones + 4 ones = ⬭ ones
Add the tens.
2 tens + 5 tens = ⬭ tens
Add the hundreds.
6 hundreds + 2 hundreds = ⬭ hundreds
So, 623 + 254 = ⬭ .

Write 623 + 254 this way.
```
  6 2 3
+ 2 5 4
```
Then add.

**Add.**
**Use base-ten blocks to help you.**

**Example**

$413 + 184 = ?$

$$\begin{array}{r} 4\ 1\ 3 \\ +\ 1\ 8\ 4 \\ \hline 597 \end{array}$$

> Add the ones first.
> Then add the tens.
> Add the hundreds last.

(6) $476 + 523 =$ 

(7) $191 + 308 =$ 

(8) Tyrone sells 445 tickets to the school fair.
Mary sells 321 tickets.
How many tickets do they sell in all? 

# Let's Practice

**Add.**

(1) 1 ten 5 ones + 3 ones = 1 ten ____ ones

(2) 3 tens 4 ones + 1 ten 5 ones = 4 tens ____ ones

(3)
$$\begin{array}{r} 2\ 7 \\ +\ 5\ 2 \\ \hline \end{array}$$

(4)
$$\begin{array}{r} 3\ 3 \\ +\ 4\ 4 \\ \hline \end{array}$$

**Add.**

(5) $16 + 3 =$ 

(6) $22 + 36 =$ 

(7) $52 + 507 =$ 

(8) $123 + 321 =$ 

**Solve.**

(9) 216 children went to Orlando on Saturday.
102 more children went on Sunday than on Saturday.
How many children went to Orlando on Sunday?

**ON YOUR OWN**

**Go to Workbook A:**
**Practice 1 and 2, pages 25–30**

# Addition with Regrouping in Ones

**Lesson Objectives**

- Use base-ten blocks to add numbers with regrouping.
- Add up to three-digit numbers with regrouping.
- Solve real-world addition problems.

**Learn** **You can add using base-ten blocks and a place-value chart to regroup ones.**

$347 + 129 = ?$

| Hundreds | Tens | Ones |
|---|---|---|
| 347 | | |
| 129 | | |

| Hundreds | Tens | Ones |
|---|---|---|
| 476 | | |

So, $347 + 129 = 476$.

**Step 1**
Add the ones.

$$
\begin{array}{r}
\overset{1}{\phantom{+}}3\ 4\ 7 \\
+\ 1\ 2\ 9 \\
\hline
6
\end{array}
$$

7 ones + 9 ones = 16 ones

**Regroup** the ones.
16 ones = 1 ten 6 ones

**Step 2**
Add the tens.

$$
\begin{array}{r}
\overset{1}{3}\ 4\ 7 \\
+\ 1\ 2\ 9 \\
\hline
7\ 6
\end{array}
$$

1 ten + 4 tens + 2 tens
= 7 tens

**Step 3**
Add the hundreds.

$$
\begin{array}{r}
\overset{1}{3}\ 4\ 7 \\
+\ 1\ 2\ 9 \\
\hline
4\ 7\ 6
\end{array}
$$

3 hundreds + 1 hundred
= 4 hundreds

## Guided Practice

**Find the missing numbers.**

**1** 136 + 127 = ?

Add the ones.

6 ones + 7 ones = ▢ ones

Regroup the ones.

▢ ones = 1 ten ▢ ones

Add the tens.

1 ten + 3 tens + 2 tens = ▢ tens

Add the hundreds.

1 hundred + 1 hundred = ▢ hundreds

So, 136 + 127 = ▢ .

Write 136 + 127 in this way.

```
   1 3 6
 + 1 2 7
_____
```

Then add.

**Add.**
**Use base-ten blocks to help you.**

**Example**

645 + 235 = ?

```
   1
  6 4 5
+ 2 3 5
_____
  880
```

5 ones + 5 ones
= 10 ones
= 1 ten

**2** 426 + 439 = ▢

**3** 706 + 274 = ▢

**4** A farmer has 318 sunflower plants.
He has 354 tomato plants.
How many plants does he have in all? ▢

# Make a Hundred!

Players: 3–4
You need:
- base ten blocks
- two ten-sided dice

 **STEP 1** Player 1 rolls the ten-sided dice. Add the numbers.

5 + 6 = 11!

**STEP 2** Take this number of 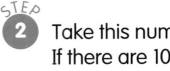. If there are 10 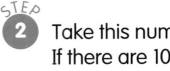, trade them for 1 ⬛⬛⬛.

11 is 1 ten and 1 one.

**STEP 3** Players take turns following **STEP 1** and **STEP 2**.

**STEP 4** After your first turn, repeat **STEP 1**.

 Take this number of . Add to the and that you have.

The first player to get 10 ⬛⬛⬛ to make a hundred square wins!

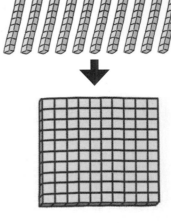

## Let's Practice

**Add.**
**Then regroup.**

**1**   4 ones + 9 ones = [    ] ones

                = [    ] ten [    ] ones

**Add.**

**2**
```
   3  1  8
+  5  2  8
_____
[          ]
```

**3**
```
   4  0  5
+  5  8  8
_____
[          ]
```

**4**   354 + 129 = [    ]

**5**   665 + 207 = [    ]

**Solve.**

**6**   637 children and 257 adults visited the zoo this morning.
How many people visited the zoo this morning?

**7**   Sam sells 162 scoops of vanilla frozen yogurt and 119 scoops
of chocolate frozen yogurt at the school fair.
How many scoops of frozen yogurt does Sam sell in all?

ON YOUR OWN

**Go to Workbook A:**
**Practice 3 and 4, pages 31–34**

# Addition with Regrouping in Tens

## Lesson Objectives

- Use base-ten blocks to add numbers with regrouping.
- Add up to three-digit numbers with regrouping.
- Solve real-world addition problems.

**Learn** **You can add using base-ten blocks and a place-value chart to regroup tens.**

$182 + 93 = ?$

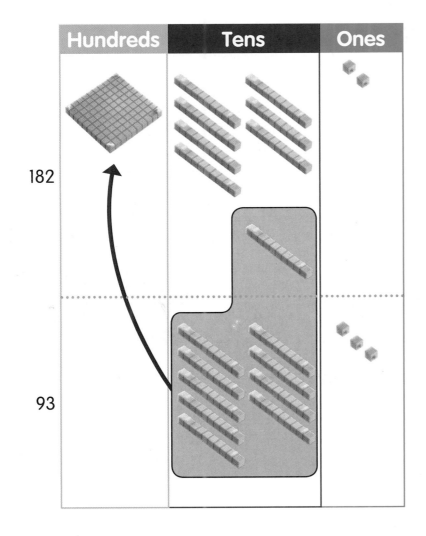

**Step 1**
Add the ones.

```
  1 8 2
+   9 3
------
      5
```

2 ones + 3 ones = 5 ones

**Step 2**
Add the tens.

```
   1
  1 8 2
+   9 3
------
    7 5
```

8 tens + 9 tens = 17 tens

Regroup the tens.

17 tens = 1 hundred 7 tens

| Hundreds | Tens | Ones |
|---|---|---|

275

So, 182 + 93 = 275.

**Step 3**
Add the hundreds.

$$
\begin{array}{r}
{\scriptstyle 1}\;\;\;\;\; \\
1\;8\;2 \\
+\;\;\;9\;3 \\
\hline
2\;7\;5
\end{array}
$$

1 hundred + 1 hundred
= 2 hundreds

# Guided Practice

**Find the missing numbers.**

**1**    361 + 170 = ?

Add the ones.

1 one + 0 ones = [ ] one

Add the tens.

6 tens + 7 tens = [ ] tens

Regroup the tens.

[ ] tens = 1 hundred [ ] tens

Add the hundreds.

1 hundred + 3 hundreds + 1 hundred = [ ] hundreds

So, 361 + 170 = [ ] .

Write 361 + 170 in this way.

$$
\begin{array}{r}
3\;6\;1 \\
+\;1\;7\;0 \\
\hline
\end{array}
$$

Then add.

## Add.
## Use base-ten blocks to help you.

**Example**

143 + 81 = ?

```
    1
   1 4 3
 +   8 1
 ───────
   2 2 4
```

4 tens + 8 tens = 12 tens
12 tens = 1 hundred 2 tens

**2**  490 + 35 = [　]

**3**  384 + 552 = [　]

## Solve.

**4**  One day, 543 cars and 274 buses pass through a toll booth. How many cars and buses pass through the toll booth in all?

[　]

# Let's Practice

## Add.
## Then regroup.

**1**  9 tens + 5 tens = [　] tens

= [　] hundred [　] tens

**2**  26 + 562 = [　]

**3**  345 + 264 = [　]

## Solve.

**4**  There are 634 boys and 281 girls in Greenland Grade School. How many students are there in all?

ON YOUR OWN

**Go to Workbook A:**
**Practice 5 and 6, pages 35–38**

# LESSON 4

# Addition with Regrouping in Ones and Tens

## Lesson Objectives

- Use base-ten blocks to add numbers with regrouping.
- Add three-digit numbers with regrouping.
- Solve real-world addition problems.

**Learn** **You can add using base-ten blocks and a place-value chart to regroup ones and tens.**

278 + 386 = ?

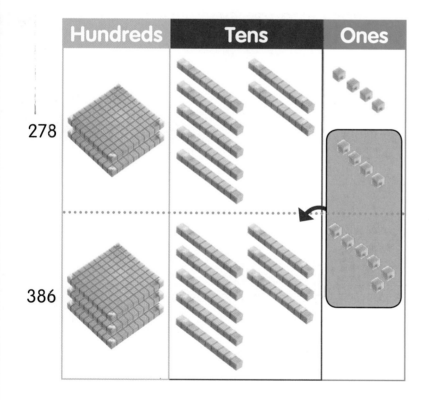

**Step 1**
Add the ones.

$$\begin{array}{r} \overset{1}{\phantom{+}2\ 7\ 8} \\ +\ 3\ 8\ 6 \\ \hline 4 \end{array}$$

8 ones + 6 ones = 14 ones

Regroup the ones.

14 ones = 1 ten 4 ones

Continued on next page

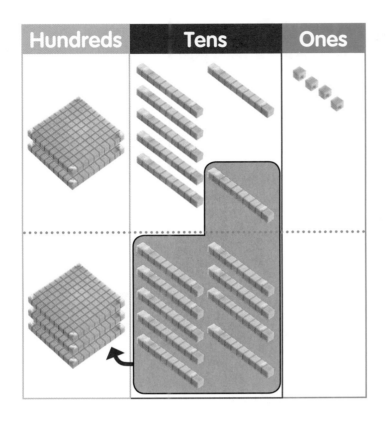

| Hundreds | Tens | Ones |
|---|---|---|

**Step 2**
Add the tens.

$$\begin{array}{r} {\overset{1}{2}}\ {\overset{1}{7}}\ 8 \\ +3\ 8\ 6 \\ \hline 6\ 4 \end{array}$$

1 ten + 7 tens + 8 tens
= 16 tens

Regroup the tens.

16 tens = 1 hundred 6 tens

| Hundreds | Tens | Ones |
|---|---|---|

664

**Step 3**
Add the hundreds.

$$\begin{array}{r} {\overset{1}{2}}\ {\overset{1}{7}}\ 8 \\ +3\ 8\ 6 \\ \hline 6\ 6\ 4 \end{array}$$

1 hundred + 2 hundreds

+ 3 hundreds = 6 hundreds

So, 278 + 386 = 664.

## Guided Practice

**Find the missing numbers.**

**1** 153 + 449 = ?

Add the ones.

3 ones + 9 ones = [ ] ones

Regroup the ones.

[ ] ones = 1 ten [ ] ones

Add the tens.

1 ten + 5 tens + 4 tens = [ ] tens

Regroup the tens.

[ ] tens = 1 hundred [ ] tens

Add the hundreds.

1 hundred + 1 hundred + 4 hundreds = [ ] hundreds

So, 153 + 449 = [ ].

Write 153 + 449 this way.

```
   1  5  3
+  4  4  9
_____
```

Then add.

**Add.**
**Use base-ten blocks to help you.**

**Example**

509 + 293 = ?

```
  1 1
  5 0 9
+ 2 9 3
_____
  802
```

Remember to change 10 ones to 1 ten and 10 tens to 1 hundred.

**2** 768 + 56 = [ ]    **3** 372 + 379 = [ ]

**Solve.**

**4** In a competition, Joan hops 125 times.
Bob hops 75 more times than Joan.
How many times does Bob hop? [ ]

# Go For The Greatest!

Players: 2–4
You need:
- three sets of number cards from 0 to 9
- pencil and paper

**STEP 1** Shuffle the cards. Each player picks six cards.

**STEP 2** Use the six cards to make as many three-digit numbers as possible. Write them down.

**STEP 3** Add any 2 three-digit numbers.
(Hint: Pick the numbers that will give the greatest answer.)
If the hundreds digits add up to more than 9, choose another number.

The player with the greatest answer wins the game!

# Let's Practice

**Find the missing numbers.**

**1** $278 + 346 = ?$

$$\begin{array}{r} 2\ 7\ 8 \\ +\ 3\ 4\ 6 \\ \hline \boxed{\phantom{000}} \end{array}$$

Add the ones.

◯ ones + ◯ ones = ◯ ones

= ◯ ten ◯ ones

Add the tens.

1 ten + ◯ tens + ◯ tens = ◯ tens

= ◯ hundred ◯ tens

Add the hundreds.

1 hundred + ◯ hundreds + ◯ hundreds = ◯ hundreds

So, $278 + 346 =$ ◯.

**Add.**

**2** $68 + 132 =$ ◯

**3** $459 + 273 =$ ◯

**4** $74 + 436 =$ ◯

**Solve.**

**5** Samantha sells 436 apples in the morning.
She sells 276 more apples in the afternoon.
How many apples does Samantha sell in the afternoon?

**6** Mr. Walsh has 784 toy cars in a box.
He puts another 96 toy cars into the box.
How many toy cars does Mr. Walsh have in
the box in all?

**7** Ray sold 468 eggs on Monday.
He sold 262 fewer eggs on
Monday than on Tuesday.
How many eggs did Ray sell on Tuesday?

He sold fewer
eggs. Do I add?

ON YOUR OWN

**Go to Workbook A:**
Practice 7 and 8, pages 39–42

## CRITICAL THINKING SKILLS
# Put On Your Thinking Cap!

**PROBLEM SOLVING**
## Find the missing numbers.

**1**

```
    1  1  1
+  ▢  ▢  ▢
─────────
    3  3  3
```

**2**

```
    4  3  2
+  4  ▢  6
─────────
    8  8  8
```

**3**

```
    1  2  ▢
+  3  4  5
─────────
    4  6  8
```

## Find the missing numbers.
## There is more than one answer.

**4**

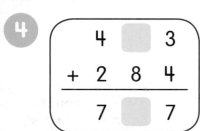

```
    4  ▢  3
+  2  8  4
─────────
    7  ▢  7
```

ON YOUR OWN

**Go to Workbook A:**
Put on Your Thinking Cap!
pages 43–44

# Chapter Wrap Up

**You have learned...**

Three-digit numbers can be added with and without regrouping.

## Addition up to 1,000

### Addition Without Regrouping

Add the ones.
Add the tens.
Add the hundreds.

$$\begin{array}{r} 2\ 4\ 6 \\ +\ 5\ 4\ 3 \\ \hline 7\ 8\ 9 \end{array}$$

### Addition with Regrouping

Regrouping in tens and ones.

Regroup.
5 ones + 7 ones
= 12 ones
= 1 ten 2 ones

$$\begin{array}{r} {}^{1}\ {}^{1}\ \ \\ 3\ 6\ 5 \\ +\ 4\ 8\ 7 \\ \hline 8\ 5\ 2 \end{array}$$

1 ten + 6 tens + 8 tens
= 15 tens
= 1 hundred 5 tens

Solve real-world addition problems.

Mrs. Grey sells 276 cookies in the morning. She sells 145 more cookies in the afternoon. How many cookies does Mrs. Grey sell in the afternoon?

She sells 421 cookies.

$$\begin{array}{r} {}^{1}\ {}^{1}\ \ \\ 2\ 7\ 6 \\ +\ 1\ 4\ 5 \\ \hline 4\ 2\ 1 \end{array}$$

**ON YOUR OWN**

**Go to Workbook A: Chapter Review/Test, pages 45–48**

# Subtraction up to 1,000

Says a thousand-legged bug
As he gives a little shrug,
"Have you seen the missing leg of mine?
If it can't be found,
I shall have to hop around,
on my other nine hundred ninety-nine."

"Hop around, hop around,
Have you seen the missing leg of mine?
If it can't be found,
I shall have to hop around,
on my other nine hundred ninety-nine."

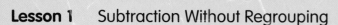

BIG IDEA

Subtract up to three-digit numbers with and without regrouping.

# Recall Prior Knowledge

## Fact family

$7 - 2 = 5$       $7 - 5 = 2$       $2 + 5 = 7$       $5 + 2 = 7$

## Adding to check subtraction

If $7 - 2 = 5$, then $5 + 2$ should equal 7.

Check your answer by adding 5 and 2.

The answer is correct.

$$\begin{array}{r} 5 \\ + 2 \\ \hline 7 \end{array}$$

## Subtracting zero

$13 - 0 = 13$            $69 - 0 = 69$

## Subtracting without regrouping

$48 - 23 = ?$

| Tens | Ones |
|------|------|

48

**Step 1**

Subtract the ones.

$$\begin{array}{cc} \text{Tens} & \text{Ones} \\ 4 & 8 \\ - \quad 2 & 3 \\ \hline & 5 \end{array}$$

8 ones – 3 ones = 5 ones

| Tens | Ones |
|------|------|

25

**Step 2**

Subtract the tens.

$$\begin{array}{cc} \text{Tens} & \text{Ones} \\ 4 & 8 \\ - \quad 2 & 3 \\ \hline 2 & 5 \end{array}$$

4 tens – 2 tens = 2 tens

So, $48 - 23 = 25$.

## Subtracting with regrouping

64 − 38 = ?

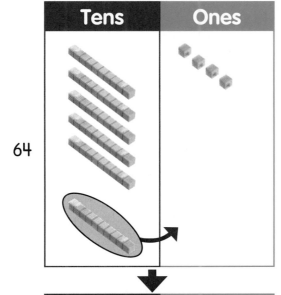

**Step 1**

Regroup the tens in 64.

64 = 6 tens 4 ones

    = 5 tens 14 ones

Subtract the ones.

| Tens | Ones |
|------|------|
| ⁵6̷ | ¹4 |
| − 3 | 8 |
| | 6 |

14 ones − 8 ones = 6 ones

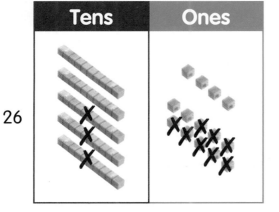

**Step 2**

Subtract the tens.

| Tens | Ones |
|------|------|
| ⁵6̷ | ¹4 |
| − 3 | 8 |
| 2 | 6 |

5 tens − 3 tens = 2 tens

So, 64 − 38 = 26.

## Subtracting to solve real-world problems

There are 12 horses in all.
8 horses are white.
How many horses are brown?

12 − 8 = 4

4 horses are brown.

✔Quick Check

**Solve.**

1 Find a subtraction sentence that belongs to the same
fact family as 14 + 5 = 19.

2 Find the addition sentence that will help you check if
56 − 3 = 53 is correct.

**Subtract.**

**3**   33 − 0 = [ ]

**4**   87 − 0 = [ ]

**Subtract.**

**5**   25 − 13 = [ ]

**6**   37 − 6 = [ ]

**Regroup the tens and ones.**
**You can use base-ten blocks to help you.**

**7**   32 = 3 tens [ ] ones

       = 2 tens [ ] ones

**Subtract.**
**You can use base-ten blocks to help you.**

**8**
```
    4  2
  − 3  3
  ───────
    [    ]
```

**9**
```
    6  7
  − 2  9
  ───────
    [    ]
```

**Solve.**

**10**   Jackie buys 24 eggs.
She drops the bag of eggs and 17 eggs break.
How many eggs are left?

[ ]

Check!
```
      1 7
  +  [    ]
  ─────────
      2 4
```

# Subtraction Without Regrouping

## Lesson Objectives

- Use base-ten blocks to subtract numbers without regrouping.
- Subtract from three-digit numbers without regrouping.
- Apply the inverse operations of addition and subtraction.
- Solve real-world subtraction problems.

## Learn You can subtract using base-ten blocks and a place-value chart.

$324 - 3 = ?$

| Hundreds | Tens | Ones |
|---|---|---|
| 324 | | |

| Hundreds | Tens | Ones |
|---|---|---|
| 321 | | |

So, $324 - 3 = 321$.

### Check!

Remember, $3 - 2 = 1$   $1 + 2 = 3$
If $324 - 3 = 321$,
then $321 + 3$ should equal 324.
The answer is correct.

$$\begin{array}{r} 3\ 2\ 1 \\ +\quad\ \ 3 \\ \hline 3\ 2\ 4 \end{array}$$

**Step 1**
Subtract the ones.

$$\begin{array}{r} 3\ 2\ 4 \\ -\quad\ \ 3 \\ \hline 1 \end{array}$$

4 ones – 3 ones = 1 one

**Step 2**
Subtract the tens.

$$\begin{array}{r} 3\ 2\ 4 \\ -\quad\ \ 3 \\ \hline 2\ 1 \end{array}$$

2 tens – 0 tens = 2 tens

**Step 3**
Subtract the hundreds.

$$\begin{array}{r} 3\ 2\ 4 \\ -\quad\ \ 3 \\ \hline 3\ 2\ 1 \end{array}$$

3 hundreds – 0 hundreds
= 3 hundreds

## You can subtract using base-ten blocks and a place-value chart.

$459 - 46 = ?$

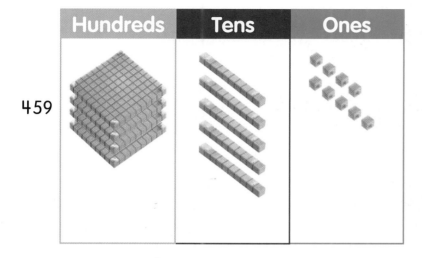

**Step 1**
Subtract the ones.

$$\begin{array}{r} 4\ 5\ \boxed{9} \\ -\quad 4\ \boxed{6} \\ \hline \boxed{3} \end{array}$$

9 ones – 6 ones = 3 ones

**Step 2**
Subtract the tens.

$$\begin{array}{r} 4\ \boxed{5}\ 9 \\ -\quad \boxed{4}\ 6 \\ \hline \boxed{1}\ 3 \end{array}$$

5 tens – 4 tens = 1 ten

**Step 3**
Subtract the hundreds.

$$\begin{array}{r} \boxed{4}\ 5\ 9 \\ -\quad\ \ 4\ 6 \\ \hline \boxed{4}\ 1\ 3 \end{array}$$

4 hundreds – 0 hundreds
= 4 hundreds

So, $459 - 46 = 413$.

### Check!

If $459 - 46 = 413$,
then $413 + 46$ should equal $459$.

$$\begin{array}{r} 4\ 1\ 3 \\ +\quad 4\ 6 \\ \hline 4\ 5\ 9 \end{array}$$

The answer is correct.

# Guided Practice

**Subtract.**
**Use base-ten blocks to help you.**
**Add to check your answer.**

**1** $408 - 6 = $ ⬭   **2** $655 - 40 = $ ⬭   **3** $348 - 27 = $ ⬭

**Learn** **You can subtract using base-ten blocks and a place-value chart.**

$249 - 134 = ?$

| Hundreds | Tens | Ones |
|---|---|---|
| 249 | | |

| Hundreds | Tens | Ones |
|---|---|---|
| 115 | | |

So, $249 - 134 = 115$.

**Check!**

If $249 - 134 = 115$,
then $115 + 134$ should equal $249$.

The answer is correct.

$$
\begin{array}{r}
1\ 1\ 5 \\
+\ 1\ 3\ 4 \\
\hline
2\ 4\ 9
\end{array}
$$

**Step 1**
Subtract the ones.

$$
\begin{array}{r}
2\ 4\ 9 \\
-\ 1\ 3\ 4 \\
\hline
5
\end{array}
$$

9 ones – 4 ones = 5 ones

**Step 2**
Subtract the tens.

$$
\begin{array}{r}
2\ 4\ 9 \\
-\ 1\ 3\ 4 \\
\hline
1\ 5
\end{array}
$$

4 tens – 3 tens = 1 ten

**Step 3**
Subtract the hundreds.

$$
\begin{array}{r}
2\ 4\ 9 \\
-\ 1\ 3\ 4 \\
\hline
1\ 1\ 5
\end{array}
$$

2 hundreds – 1 hundred
= 1 hundred

## Guided Practice

**Find the missing numbers.**

**4**   327 – 115 = ?

Subtract the ones.

7 ones – 5 ones = ⬚ ones

Subtract the tens.

2 tens – 1 ten = ⬚ ten

Subtract the hundreds.

3 hundreds – 1 hundred = 2 hundreds

So, 327 – 115 = ⬚.

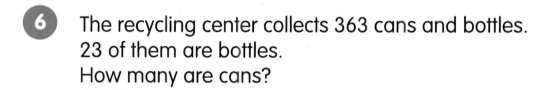

Write 327 – 115 this way.

```
    3 2 7
 –  1 1 5
 _____
```

Then subtract.

**Check!**

```
      ⬚
 +  1 1 5
 _____
    3 2 7
```

**Solve.**

**5**   There are 128 apples in a barrel.
5 of the apples are rotten.
How many apples are not rotten?

⬚

**6**   The recycling center collects 363 cans and bottles.
23 of them are bottles.
How many are cans?

⬚

**7**   There are 999 adults at a concert.
447 of them are men.
How many are women?

⬚

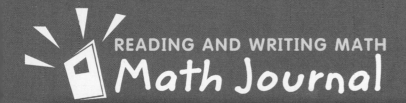

758 − 35 = 732

Is the answer correct?
Explain why you think so.
Show how you would check it.

# Let's Practice

**Subtract.**

**1** 4 tens 8 ones − 5 ones = 4 tens ⬜ ones

**2** 7 tens 9 ones − 3 tens 2 ones = ⬜ tens 7 ones

**Subtract.**

**3**
```
    7  8
 −  2  4
 _____
   ⬜
```

**4**
```
    9  8
 −  5  6
 _____
   ⬜
```

**Subtract.**

**5** 38 − 15 = ⬜   **6** 77 − 24 = ⬜   **7** 97 − 3 = ⬜

**Subtract.**
**Use base-ten blocks to help you.**

**Example**

$$398 - 253 = \boxed{145}$$

$$\begin{array}{r} 3\ 9\ 8 \\ -\ 2\ 5\ 3 \\ \hline 1\ 4\ 5 \end{array}$$

Subtract the ones first. Then subtract the tens. Remember to subtract the hundreds last.

**8**    $564 - 321 = \boxed{\phantom{000}}$

**9**    $683 - 532 = \boxed{\phantom{000}}$

**10**    $475 - 54 = \boxed{\phantom{000}}$

**Solve.**
**Show how to check your answer.**

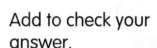

Add to check your answer.

**11**    There are 687 boxes of cereal at a store.
324 of them have toys inside.
How many cereal boxes do not have toys inside?

**12**    Ramon has 798 trading cards.
He gives 265 of them to his sister.
How many trading cards does he have left?

ON YOUR OWN

**Go to Workbook A:**
**Practice 1 and 2, pages 49–52**

# LESSON
# 2 Subtraction with Regrouping in Tens and Ones

## Lesson Objectives

- Use base-ten blocks to subtract with regrouping.
- Subtract from three-digit numbers with regrouping.
- Apply the inverse operations of addition and subtraction.
- Solve real-world subtraction problems.

**Learn** **You can subtract using base-ten blocks and a place-value chart to regroup tens and ones.**

$242 - 128 = ?$

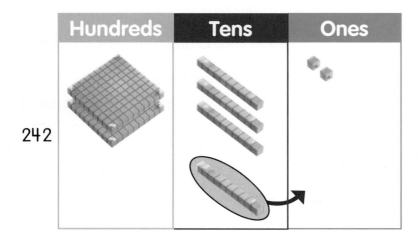

**Step 1**

You cannot subtract 8 ones from 2 ones. So, regroup the tens and ones.

Subtract the ones. Regroup the tens and ones in 242.

$$
\begin{array}{r}
2 \; \overset{3}{\cancel{4}} \; \overset{1}{2} \\
- \; 1 \; 2 \; 8 \\
\hline
\end{array}
$$

4 tens 2 ones
= 3 tens 12 ones

Continued on next page

| Hundreds | Tens | Ones |
|---|---|---|

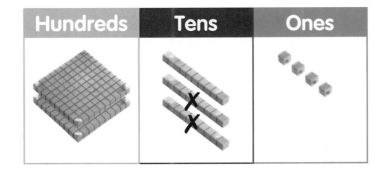

Subtract.

$$\begin{array}{r} 2 \ \overset{3}{\cancel{4}} \ {}^{1}2 \\ -\ 1 \ \ 2 \ \ 8 \\ \hline 4 \end{array}$$

12 ones − 8 ones = 4 ones

| Hundreds | Tens | Ones |
|---|---|---|

**Step 2**
Subtract the tens.

$$\begin{array}{r} 2 \ \overset{3}{\cancel{4}} \ {}^{1}2 \\ -\ 1 \ \ 2 \ \ 8 \\ \hline 1 \ \ 4 \end{array}$$

3 tens − 2 tens = 1 ten

114

| Hundreds | Tens | Ones |
|---|---|---|

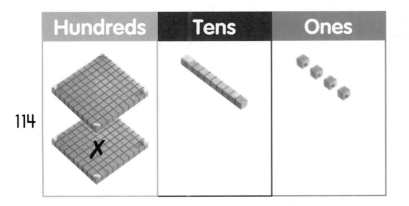

**Step 3**
Subtract the hundreds.

$$\begin{array}{r} 2 \ \overset{3}{\cancel{4}} \ {}^{1}2 \\ -\ 1 \ \ 2 \ \ 8 \\ \hline 1 \ \ 1 \ \ 4 \end{array}$$

2 hundreds − 1 hundred
= 1 hundred

So, 242 − 128 = 114.

## Check!

If 242 − 128 = 114,
then 114 + 128 should
equal 242.

The answer is correct.

$$\begin{array}{r} {}^{1}\phantom{1} \\ 1 \ \ 1 \ \ 4 \\ +\ 1 \ \ 2 \ \ 8 \\ \hline 2 \ \ 4 \ \ 2 \end{array}$$

## Guided Practice

**1**  **Find the missing numbers.**

763 − 207 = ?

Subtract the ones.
Regroup the tens and ones.

63 = 6 tens ⬜ ones

  = 5 tens ⬜ ones

Subtract.

⬜ ones − ⬜ ones = ⬜ ones

Subtract the tens.
5 tens − 0 tens = ⬜ tens

Subtract the hundreds.
7 hundreds − 2 hundreds
= ⬜ hundreds

So, 763 − 207 = ⬜ .

Write 763 − 207 this way.

```
   7 6 3
 − 2 0 7
 ───────
```

Then subtract.

**Check!**

```
     ⬜
 + 2 0 7
 ───────
   7 6 3
```

**Subtract.**
**Use base-ten blocks to help you.**
**Add to check your answer.**

**Example**

```
      8
   2  9  ¹1
 −    5  5
 ─────────
   2  3  6
```

Remember to regroup
the tens and ones.

**2**
```
     5 4 8
   − 3 1 9
   ───────
     ⬜
```

**3**
```
     9 7 7
   − 4 5 9
   ───────
     ⬜
```

**Solve.**

**4** Tara is in the skipping contest at field day.
She must skip 255 times without stopping.
She has skipped 128 times without stopping.
How many more times must she skip?

**5** Mr. Sanchez has an 835-page book.
He has read 219 pages.
How many more pages does he have to read?

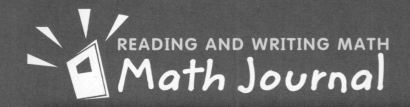

### READING AND WRITING MATH
## Math Journal

**1** $732 - 218 = 516$
Is the answer correct?
Show how you would check it.

**Tell how you could solve this problem.**
**Then solve it.**
**How could you check your answer?**

**2** There are 781 rooms in a hotel.
472 rooms are white.
The rest are blue.
How many rooms are blue?

# Let's Practice

**Regroup the tens and ones.**
**Use base-ten blocks to help you.**

**1** 142 = 1 hundred 4 tens [ ] ones

    = 1 hundred 3 tens [ ] ones

**2** 570 = 5 hundreds 7 tens [ ] ones

    = 5 hundreds 6 tens [ ] ones

**3** 612 = 6 hundreds [ ] ten 2 ones

    = 6 hundreds [ ] tens 12 ones

**Subtract.**
**Use base-ten blocks to help you.**

**4**
```
    8 8 0
 -  6 5 6
```
[ ]

**5**
```
    9 9 2
 -  8 7 9
```
[ ]

Add to check
your answer.

**6**
```
    7 8 3
 -    6 9
```
[ ]

**7**
```
    4 1 6
 -  3 0 7
```
[ ]

**Solve.**
**Show how to check your answer.**

**8** A castle tower has 283 steps.
Jake climbs 77 steps.
How many more steps must he climb to reach the top?

**9** Movie Theater A has 407 seats.
Movie Theater B has 673 seats.
How many more seats does Movie
Theater B have than Movie Theater A?

ON YOUR OWN

Go to Workbook A:
Practice 3 and 4, pages 53–56

# LESSON
# 3 Subtraction with Regrouping in Hundreds and Tens

## Lesson Objectives

- Use base-ten blocks to subtract with regrouping.
- Subtract from a three-digit number with regrouping.
- Apply the inverse operations of addition and subtraction.
- Solve real-world subtraction problems.

**Learn** **You can subtract using base-ten blocks and a place-value chart to regroup hundreds and tens.**

$537 - 272 = ?$

| Hundreds | Tens | Ones |
|---|---|---|
| 537 | | |

**Step 1**
Subtract the ones.

$$\begin{array}{r} 5\ 3\ 7 \\ -\ 2\ 7\ 2 \\ \hline 5 \end{array}$$

7 ones – 2 ones = 5 ones

**Step 2**
Subtract the tens.

$$\begin{array}{r} 5\ ?3\ 7 \\ -\ 2\ 7\ 2 \\ \hline 5 \end{array}$$

You cannot subtract 7 tens from 3 tens.
So, regroup the hundreds and tens.

| Hundreds | Tens | Ones |
|---|---|---|

Regroup the hundreds and tens in 537.

$$\begin{array}{r} \overset{4}{\cancel{5}}\,{}^{1}3\ 7 \\ -\ 2\ 7\ 2 \\ \hline 6\ 5 \end{array}$$

5 hundreds 3 tens
= 4 hundreds 13 tens

| Hundreds | Tens | Ones |
|---|---|---|

Remember to regroup when you do not have enough to subtract.

| Hundreds | Tens | Ones |
|---|---|---|

Subtract.

$$\begin{array}{r} \overset{4}{\cancel{5}}\,{}^{1}3\ 7 \\ -\ 2\ 7\ 2 \\ \hline 6\ 5 \end{array}$$

13 tens − 7 tens = 6 tens

Continued on next page

**Lesson 3**  Subtraction with Regrouping in Hundreds and Tens  **73**

| Hundreds | Tens | Ones |
|----------|------|------|

265

So, 537 − 272 = 265.

**Step 3**

Subtract the hundreds.

```
  4
  5̷ ¹3 7
−  2  7 2
   2  6 5
```

4 hundreds − 2 hundreds
= 2 hundreds

## Check!

If 537 − 272 = 265,
then 265 + 272 should
equal 537.

The answer is correct.

```
      1
    2  6  5
 +  2  7  2
    5  3  7
```

# Guided Practice

**1** **Find the missing numbers.**

719 − 383 = ?

Subtract the ones.

9 ones − 3 ones = ⬭ ones

> Write 719 − 383 this way.
>
> ```
>    7  1  9
> −  3  8  3
> ─────────
> ```
>
> Then subtract.

Subtract the tens.
Regroup the hundreds and tens.
7 hundreds 1 ten = 6 hundreds ⬭ tens

Subtract.

◯ tens − ◯ tens = ◯ tens

Subtract the hundreds.

6 hundreds − 3 hundreds = ◯ hundreds.

So, 719 − 383 = ◯ .

Check!

```
    ◯
+ 3 8 3
───────
  7 1 9
```

## Subtract.
## Use base-ten blocks to help you.

**2**
```
  6 4 7
− 2 6 7
───────
```
◯

**3**
```
  9 1 5
− 8 2 4
───────
```
◯

**4**
```
  3 3 6
− 1 5 4
───────
```
◯

## Solve.

**5** Aisha has 235 stickers.
Pedro has 153 fewer stickers than Aisha.
How many stickers does Pedro have? ◯

**6** A baker made 306 rolls in the morning.
256 rolls are sold during the day.
How many rolls are left? ◯

# Break a Hundred!

Players: 3–4
You need:
- two ten-sided dice
- base-ten blocks

**STEP 1** Decide who will be the banker.

**STEP 2** Players get 1  each from the banker.

**STEP 3** Each player trades  for 9 ▭▭▭ and 10 ▪.

**STEP 4** Player 1 rolls the ten-sided dice. He takes away this number of ▪ from his ▭▭▭ and ▪.

**STEP 5** Players take turns. Players trade 1 ▭▭▭ for ▪ if they need to.

The first player to give away all the ▪ and ▭▭▭ wins!

# Let's Practice

**Regroup the hundreds and tens.**
**Use base-ten blocks to help you.**

**1**  569 = 4 hundreds ⬚ tens 9 ones

**2**  606 = ⬚ hundreds 10 tens 6 ones

**Subtract.**
**Use addition to check your answer.**

**3**
```
    5 2 9
  - 3 7 5
```
⬚

**4**
```
    4 0 8
  - 1 6 4
```
⬚

**5**
```
    8 5 7
  - 3 8 5
```
⬚

**6**  853 − 791 = ⬚

**7**  589 − 493 = ⬚

**8**  604 − 311 = ⬚

**Use addition to check if the answers are correct.**

**9**  True or false? 827 − 564 = 343  ⬚

**10**  True or false? 705 − 293 = 592  ⬚

**Solve.**
**Show how to check your answer.**

**11**  648 people visit a carnival.
295 are adults.
How many are children?

**12**  953 students are in King Elementary School.
492 students are in Lamar Elementary School.
How many more students are in King Elementary
School than in Lamar Elementary School?

ON YOUR OWN

Go to Workbook A:
Practice 5 and 6, pages 57–60

# LESSON 4

# Subtraction with Regrouping in Hundreds, Tens, and Ones

**Lesson Objectives**

- Use base-ten blocks to subtract with regrouping.
- Subtract from a three-digit number with regrouping.
- Apply the inverse operations of addition and subtraction.
- Solve real-world subtraction problems.

**Learn** **You can subtract using base-ten blocks and a place-value chart to regroup hundreds, tens, and ones.**

432 – 178 = ?

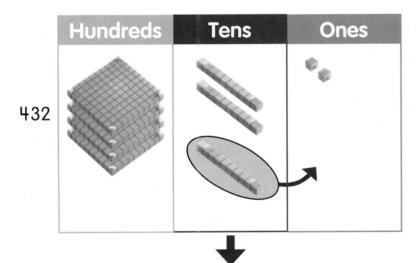

**Step 1**
Subtract the ones.

You cannot subtract 8 ones from 2 ones. So, regroup the tens and ones.

Regroup the tens and ones in 432.

$$
\begin{array}{r}
4\ \overset{2}{\cancel{3}}\ ^{1}2 \\
-\ 1\ 7\ 8 \\
\hline
\end{array}
$$

3 tens 2 ones
= 2 tens 12 ones

| Hundreds | Tens | Ones |
|---|---|---|

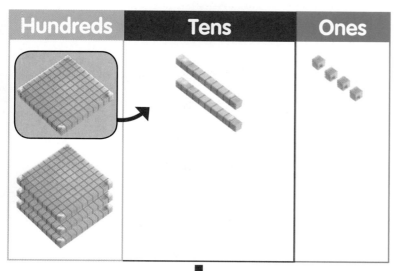

Subtract.

$$\begin{array}{r} \overset{\hspace{1.2em}2}{4\ \cancel{3}\ |^{1}2} \\ -\ 1\ 7\ |\ 8 \\ \hline |\ 4 \end{array}$$

12 ones − 8 ones = 4 ones

| Hundreds | Tens | Ones |
|---|---|---|

**Step 2**

Subtract the tens.

You cannot subtract 7 tens from 2 tens. So, regroup the hundreds and tens.

| Hundreds | Tens | Ones |
|---|---|---|

Regroup the hundreds and tens in 432.

$$\begin{array}{r} \overset{3\ \ \ ^{1}2}{4\ \cancel{3}\ \ ^{1}2} \\ -\ 1\ 7\ \ 8 \\ \hline 4 \end{array}$$

4 hundreds 2 tens
= 3 hundreds 12 tens

Continued on next page

| Hundreds | Tens | Ones |
|----------|------|------|

Subtract.

$$
\begin{array}{r}
\overset{3}{\cancel{4}}\overset{\cancel{12}}{\cancel{3}}\,^{1}2 \\
-\ 1\ 7\ 8 \\
\hline
5\ 4
\end{array}
$$

12 tens – 7 tens = 5 tens

| Hundreds | Tens | Ones |
|----------|------|------|

254

## Step 3

Subtract the hundreds.

$$
\begin{array}{r}
\overset{3}{\cancel{4}}\ \overset{\cancel{12}}{\cancel{3}}\,^{1}2 \\
-\ 1\ 7\ 8 \\
\hline
2\ 5\ 4
\end{array}
$$

3 hundreds – 1 hundred
= 2 hundreds

So, 432 – 178 = 254.

### Check!

If 432 – 178 = 254,
then 254 + 178 should
equal 432.

The answer is correct.

$$
\begin{array}{r}
{}^{1}\ {}^{1}\ \\
2\ 5\ 4 \\
+\ 1\ 7\ 8 \\
\hline
4\ 3\ 2
\end{array}
$$

## Guided Practice

### Find the missing numbers.

**1**  235 − 149 = ?

Subtract the ones.
Regroup the tens and ones.

3 tens 5 ones = 2 tens [ ] ones

Subtract.

[ ] ones − [ ] ones = [ ] ones

Subtract the tens.
Regroup the hundreds and tens.

2 hundreds 2 tens = 1 hundred [ ] tens

Subtract.

[ ] tens − [ ] tens = [ ] tens

Subtract the hundreds.

1 hundred − 1 hundred = [ ] hundreds

So, 235 − 149 = [ ] .

Write 235 − 149 this way.

```
    2 3 5
  − 1 4 9
  ─────────
```

Then subtract.

**Check!**

```
      [ ]
  +  1 4 9
  ─────────
     2 3 5
```

## Subtract.

**2**
```
    5 3 2
  − 3 7 9
  ─────────
    [ ]
```

**3**
```
    6 7 3
  − 1 9 8
  ─────────
    [ ]
```

**Solve.**

**4** There are 612 boys in East School.
There are 138 fewer girls in the school.
How many girls are there?

# Let's Practice

**Find the missing numbers.**
**Use base-ten blocks to help you.**

**1** 5 hundreds = 4 hundreds ⬚ tens

= 4 hundreds ⬚ tens 10 ones

**2** 8 hundreds = 7 hundreds ⬚ tens

= 7 hundreds ⬚ tens 10 ones

**Regroup hundreds, tens, and ones.**
**Use base-ten blocks to help you.**

**3** 326 = 3 hundreds 2 tens ⬚ ones

= 3 hundreds 1 ten ⬚ ones

= 2 hundreds ⬚ tens ⬚ ones

**4** 517 = 5 hundreds ⬚ ten 7 ones

= 4 hundreds ⬚ tens 7 ones

= 4 hundreds ⬚ tens ⬚ ones

## Subtract.

**5**
```
    8 2 4
  – 5 6 8
```
[ ]

**6**
```
    8 1 2
  – 2 3 8
```
[ ]

**7** 673 – 498 = [ ]

**8** 317 – 289 = [ ]

## Solve.
## Show how to check your answer.

**9** Your school library has 746 books.
289 books are new.
How many books are not new?

**10** Mrs. Jones uses 365 beads to make a purse.
She uses 296 beads to make a necklace.
How many more beads does she use to make the purse?

**11** A flower shop has 724 yellow tulips.
It has 28 fewer orange tulips.
How many orange tulips are there?

ON YOUR OWN

Go to Workbook A:
Practice 7 and 8, pages 61–64

# Subtraction Across Zeros

## Lesson Objectives

- Use base-ten blocks to show subtraction with regrouping.
- Subtract from a three-digit number with regrouping.
- Apply the inverse operations of addition and subtraction.
- Solve real-world subtraction problems.

**Learn** **You can subtract from numbers with zeros using base-ten blocks and a place-value chart.**

$200 - 18 = ?$

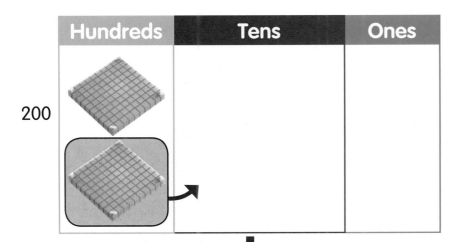

**Step 1**
Subtract the ones. Regroup the hundreds and tens.

$$\begin{array}{r} {}^{1}\cancel{2}\,{}^{1}0\ 0 \\ -\ \ 1\ 8 \\ \hline \end{array}$$

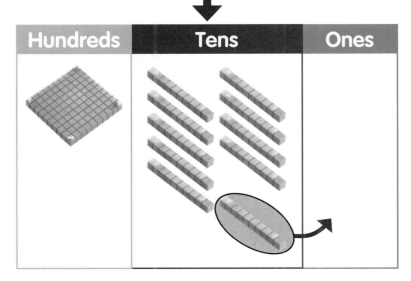

Regroup the tens and ones.

$$\begin{array}{r} {}^{1}\ \ {}^{9} \\ \cancel{2}\ {}^{\cancel{0}}\,{}^{1}0 \\ -\ \ \ 1\ 8 \\ \hline \end{array}$$

2 hundreds
= 1 hundred 10 tens
= 1 hundred 9 tens
   10 ones

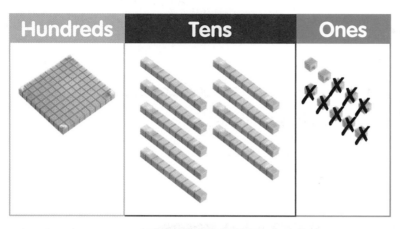

Subtract.

$$\begin{array}{r} \overset{1}{\cancel{2}}\,\overset{9}{\cancel{0}}\,{}^{1}0 \\ -\quad 1\ 8 \\ \hline 2 \end{array}$$

10 ones − 8 ones = 2 ones

## Step 2

Subtract the tens.

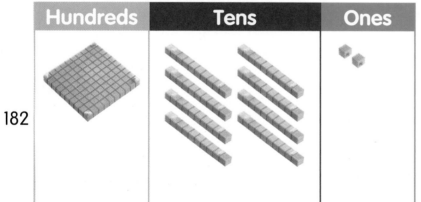

$$\begin{array}{r} \overset{1}{\cancel{2}}\,\overset{9}{\cancel{0}}\,{}^{1}0 \\ -\quad 1\ 8 \\ \hline 8\ 2 \end{array}$$

9 tens − 1 ten = 8 tens

## Step 3

Subtract the hundreds.

182

$$\begin{array}{r} \overset{1}{\cancel{2}}\,\overset{9}{\cancel{0}}\,{}^{1}0 \\ -\quad 1\ 8 \\ \hline 1\ 8\ 2 \end{array}$$

1 hundred − 0 hundreds
= 1 hundred

So, 200 − 18 = 182.

## Check!

If 200 − 18 = 182, then
182 + 18 should equal 200.

The answer is correct.

$$\begin{array}{r} \overset{1}{\ }\ \overset{1}{\ }\ \\ 1\ 8\ 2 \\ +\quad 1\ 8 \\ \hline 2\ 0\ 0 \end{array}$$

## Guided Practice

### Find the missing numbers.

 **1**  300 − 72 = ?

Subtract the ones.
Regroup the hundreds, tens, and ones.
3 hundreds = 2 hundreds ⬜ tens

            = 2 hundreds ⬜ tens 10 ones

Subtract.
⬜ ones − ⬜ ones = ⬜ ones

Subtract the tens.
⬜ tens − ⬜ tens = ⬜ tens

Subtract the hundreds.
⬜ hundreds − ⬜ hundreds = ⬜ hundreds

So, 300 − 72 = ⬜.

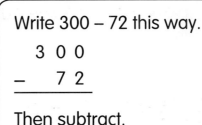

Write 300 − 72 this way.

$$\begin{array}{r} 3\ 0\ 0 \\ -\ \ \ 7\ 2 \\ \hline \end{array}$$

Then subtract.

### Subtract.
### Use base-ten blocks to help you.

**Example**

$$\begin{array}{r} \overset{4}{\cancel{5}}\ \overset{9}{\cancel{\cancel{0}}}\ {}^{1}0 \\ -\ 2\ 6\ 7 \\ \hline 2\ 3\ 3 \end{array}$$

**2**
$$\begin{array}{r} 1\ 0\ 0 \\ -\ \ \ 9\ 8 \\ \hline \end{array}$$
⬜

**3**
$$\begin{array}{r} 6\ 0\ 0 \\ -\ 3\ 0\ 8 \\ \hline \end{array}$$
⬜

### Solve.

 **4**  Dan has 200 baseball cards.
He gives away 24 baseball cards.
How many baseball cards are left? ⬜

**5**  Baker Anne has 300 cookie cutters.
127 cookie cutters are in the shape of bunnies.
How many cookie cutters are not in the shape of bunnies?

# Let's Practice

**Find the missing numbers.**

**1**  300 = 2 hundreds ⬭ tens 0 ones

= 2 hundreds ⬭ tens 10 ones

**2**  700 = 6 hundreds ⬭ tens 0 ones

= 6 hundreds ⬭ tens 10 ones

**3**  800 = ⬭ hundreds 10 tens ⬭ ones

= ⬭ hundreds ⬭ tens 10 ones

**4**
```
  3 0 0
– 2 5 4
```

**5**
```
  9 0 0
– 7 3 4
```

**6**
```
  6 0 0
– 3 4 5
```

**Subtract.**
**Use base-ten blocks to help you.**

**7**  400 – 98

**8**  500 – 487

**9**  700 – 402

**Solve.**
**Show how to check your answer.**

**10**  Misha scores 400 points in a computer game.
Her brother scores 189 points in the same game.
How many more points does Misha score
than her brother?

ON YOUR OWN

Go to Workbook A:
Practice 9, pages 65–66

# Put On Your Thinking Cap!

**PROBLEM SOLVING**

## Find the missing numbers in each box.

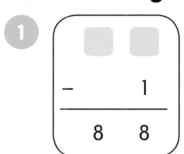

1

```
    ▢  ▢
 -     1
 ───────
    8  8
```

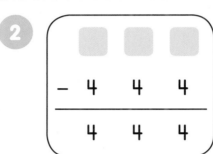

2

```
    ▢  ▢  ▢
 -  4  4  4
 ──────────
    4  4  4
```

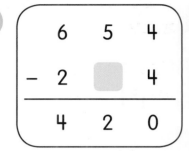

3

```
    6  5  4
 -  2  ▢  4
 ──────────
    4  2  0
```

## Answer the question.

4  Brian has a machine that changes numbers.
He puts one number into the machine and a different
number comes out.
When he puts 12 into the machine, the number 7 comes out.
When he puts 20 into the machine, the number 15 comes out.
The table on page 89 shows his results for 4 numbers.

Write the rule the machine uses to change the numbers. Then, find the two missing numbers.

Use the example below to help you.

| Number in | Number out |
|---|---|
| 12 | 7 |
| 20 | 15 |
| 49 | 44 |
| 82 | 77 |
| 100 | |
| | 200 |

**Example**

| Number in | Number out |
|---|---|
| 4 | 6 |
| 7 | 9 |
| 10 | 12 |
| 19 | 2 1 |

6 is 2 more than 4, 9 is 2 more than 7, 12 is 2 more than 10. So, the rule is to add 2 to the number put in.

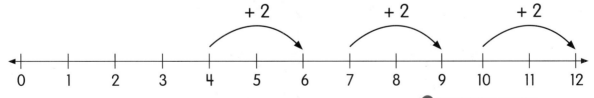

$+2$     $+2$     $+2$

Rule: + 2 to the number put in.

**ON YOUR OWN**

Go to Workbook A:
Put on Your Thinking Cap!
pages 67–68

# Chapter Wrap Up

**You have learned...**

## Subtraction up to 1,000

### Subtraction without regrouping

Subtract the ones.
Subtract the tens.
Subtract the hundreds.

$$\begin{array}{r} 8\ 7\ 6 \\ -\ 2\ 3\ 4 \\ \hline 6\ 4\ 2 \end{array}$$

Check using addition.
If 876 – 234 = 642,
then 642 + 234
should equal 876.

$$\begin{array}{r} 6\ 4\ 2 \\ +\ 2\ 3\ 4 \\ \hline 8\ 7\ 6 \end{array}$$

The answer is correct.

### Subtraction with regrouping

Regrouping in tens and ones.

Regroup.
987 = 9 hundreds 8 tens
      7 ones
  = 9 hundreds 7 tens
     17 ones

$$\begin{array}{r} 9\ \overset{7}{\cancel{8}}\ {}^{1}7 \\ -\ 1\ 2\ 9 \\ \hline 8\ 5\ 8 \end{array}$$

Check using addition.
If 987 – 129 = 858,
then 858 + 129 should
equal 987.

$$\begin{array}{r} 8\ \overset{1}{5}\ 8 \\ +\ 1\ 2\ 9 \\ \hline 9\ 8\ 7 \end{array}$$

The answer is correct.

---

Solve real-world subtraction problems.

A bakery sells 347 loaves of bread on Sunday.
It sells 168 fewer loaves of bread on Monday.
How many loaves of bread does the bakery sell on Monday?

347 – 168 = 179

$$\begin{array}{r} \overset{2}{\cancel{3}}\ {}^{1}\overset{3}{\cancel{4}}\ {}^{1}7 \\ -\ 1\ 6\ 8 \\ \hline 1\ 7\ 9 \end{array}$$

The bakery sells 179 loaves of bread on Monday.

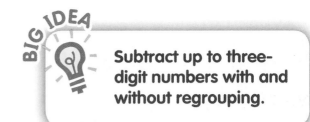

BIG IDEA

Subtract up to three-digit numbers with and without regrouping.

Regrouping in hundreds and tens.

$$\begin{array}{r} \overset{8}{\cancel{9}}\,{}^{1}4\;6 \\ -\;\;2\;5\;3 \\ \hline 6\;9\;3 \end{array}$$

Regroup.
946 = 9 hundreds 4 tens 6 ones
= 8 hundreds 14 tens 6 ones

Check using addition.
If 946 − 253 = 693,
then 693 + 253 should
equal 946.

$$\begin{array}{r} {}^{1}6\;9\;3 \\ +\;2\;5\;3 \\ \hline 9\;4\;6 \end{array}$$

The answer is correct.

Regrouping in hundreds, tens, and ones.

$$\begin{array}{r} \overset{5}{\cancel{6}}\;\overset{9}{\cancel{0}}\,{}^{1}0 \\ -\;\;4\;8\;7 \\ \hline 1\;1\;3 \end{array}$$

Regroup.
600 = 6 hundreds
= 5 hundreds 10 tens
= 5 hundreds 9 tens
10 ones

Check using addition.
If 600 − 487 = 113,
then 113 + 487 should
equal 600.

$$\begin{array}{r} {}^{1}1\;{}^{1}1\;3 \\ +\;4\;8\;7 \\ \hline 6\;0\;0 \end{array}$$

The answer is correct.

ON YOUR OWN

**Go to Workbook A:**
**Chapter Review/Test,**
**pages 69–72**

# CHAPTER 4

# Using Bar Models: Addition and Subtraction

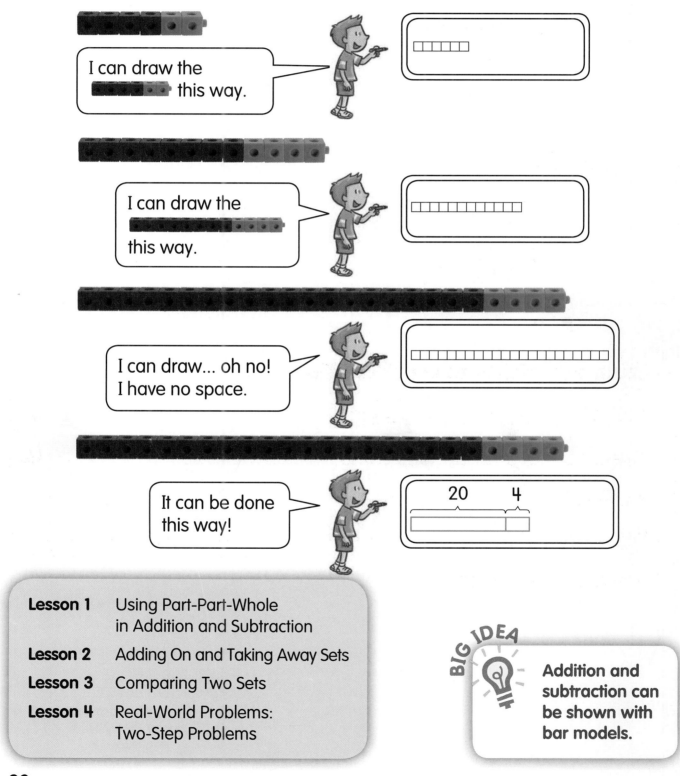

I can draw the ■■■■■■ this way.

I can draw the ■■■■■■■ this way.

I can draw... oh no! I have no space.

It can be done this way!

20    4

**BIG IDEA**

Addition and subtraction can be shown with bar models.

## Recall Prior Knowledge

### Adding and subtracting numbers

**1** Without regrouping

a
```
   2 3 5
 + 3 2 4
 -------
   5 5 9
```

b
```
   5 7 9
 - 2 4 5
 -------
   3 3 4
```

**2** With regrouping

a
```
    ¹ ¹
   4 2 7
 + 1 8 5
 -------
   6 1 2
```

b
```
    7 ¹1
   8 2 ¹5
 - 3 6 7
 -------
   4 5 8
```

### Using subtraction to check addition

In **2** **a** above, $427 + 185 = 612$.

Check your answer by subtracting.

$612 - 185 = 427$ or

$612 - 427 = 185$

The answer is correct.

**Check!**
```
    5  ¹0
   6  1  ¹2
 - 1  8  5
 ---------
   4  2  7
```

**Check!**
```
    5  ¹0
   6  1  ¹2
 - 4  2  7
 ---------
   1  8  5
```

## Solving addition and subtraction problems

**1**    A farmer has 28 chicks and 32 ducklings.
How many chicks and ducklings does he have in all?

28 + 32 = 60

The farmer has 60 chicks and ducklings in all.

**2**    Our teacher has 50 pens and pencils.
28 of them are pens.
How many pencils are there?

50 − 28 = 22

There are 22 pencils.

**3**    Jim has 56 pennies in his piggy bank.
His mother puts 17 more pennies into the bank.
How many pennies does he have now?

56 + 17 = 73

He has 73 pennies now.

**4**    Mr. Armstrong bakes 92 muffins.
He sells 38 of them.
How many muffins does he have left?

92 − 38 = 54

He has 54 muffins left.

## ✔ Quick Check

**Add or subtract.**

① 
```
    4 5 7
  + 3 4 2
  _____
```

② 
```
    7 3 9
  - 6 1 8
  _____
```

③ 
```
    2 6 8
  + 5 9 7
  _____
```

④ 
```
    5 0 0
  - 2 2 5
  _____
```

**Check!**

```
  +   2 2 5
  _____
      5 0 0
```

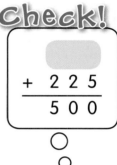

**Solve.**

⑤ Pepe has 45 stickers of cars.
He has 37 stickers of planes.
How many stickers does he have in all?

⑥ The Art Club has 85 members.
66 are girls.
How many are boys?

⑦ Carl has 36 swimming medals.
He wins another 15 swimming medals this year.
How many medals does he have now?

⑧ Mrs. Gordon has 68 balloons.
She gives away 29 balloons.
How many balloons does she have now?

## LESSON 1 Using Part-Part-Whole in Addition and Subtraction

**Lesson Objectives**

- Use bar models to solve addition and subtraction problems.
- Apply the inverse operations of addition and subtraction.

**Learn** **You can use bar models to help you add.**

Mandy makes 10 granola bars.
Aida makes 12 granola bars.
How many granola bars do they make in all?

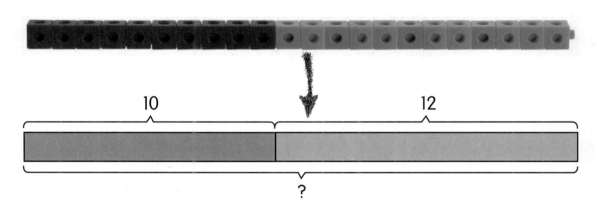

10 + 12 = 22

They make 22 granola bars in all.

22 − 10 = 12
22 − 12 = 10
The answer is correct.

# Guided Practice

**Find the missing numbers.**
**Use the bar model to help you.**

**1** Helen puts 14 breadsticks in a basket.
Her friend puts 17 breadsticks in the basket.
How many breadsticks are in the basket?

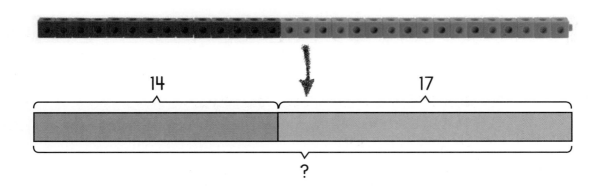

14              17

?

[ ]  +  [ ]  =  [ ]

There are [ ] breadsticks in the basket.

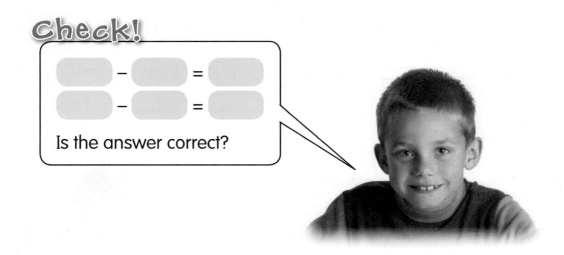

**Check!**

[ ]  −  [ ]  =  [ ]
[ ]  −  [ ]  =  [ ]

Is the answer correct?

# You can use bar models to help you subtract.

Will buys 24 eggs.
He breaks 7 eggs.
How many eggs do not break?

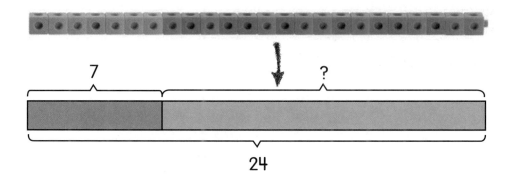

7       ?

24

24 − 7 = 17

17 eggs do not break.

**Check!**

17 + 7 = 24

The answer is correct.

# Guided Practice

**Find the missing numbers.**
**Use the bar model to help you.**

**2** The second grade class has a new aquarium.
There are 21 fish in it.
15 fish were given by families.
The rest were bought by the school.
How many fish did the school buy?

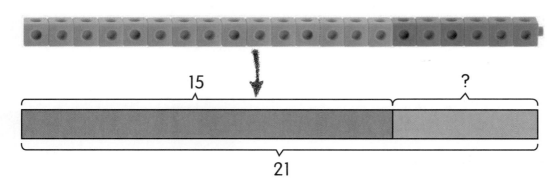

⬭ − ⬭ = ⬭

The school bought ⬭ fish.

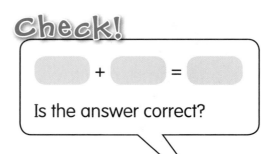

**Check!**

⬭ + ⬭ = ⬭

Is the answer correct?

# Hands-On Activity

Write a favorite name, a number less than 20, and the name of a favorite toy on three pieces of paper. Your classmates will do the same.

STEP 2

Your teacher has three bags. They are labeled as shown. Drop each piece of paper into the correct bag.

STEP 3

Pick one name, one toy and two numbers from the bags.

STEP 4

Write a real-world problem using the words and numbers that you picked.

Return the pieces of paper that you have picked into the correct bags.

Read your real-world problem to your classmates. Have them show your real-world problem with bar models.

**Example**

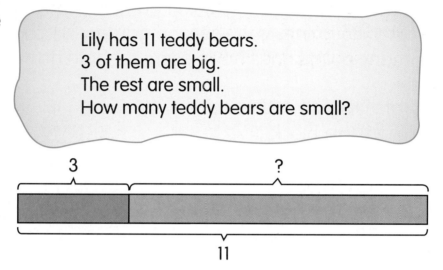

Lily has 11 teddy bears.
3 of them are big.
The rest are small.
How many teddy bears are small?

Take turns picking papers from the bags and writing real-world problems.

# Guided Practice

**Solve.**
**Use bar models to help you.**

**3** The library spends $225 on books.
It has $78 left to spend.
How much does the library have at first?

**4** The art teacher has $745.
She buys paint supplies for $257.
She spends the rest of the money on drawing supplies.
How much do the drawing supplies cost?

## Let's Practice

**Solve.**
**Draw bar models to help you.**

**1** Kevin scores 78 points in the first game he bowls.
He scores 85 points in the second game.
How many points does Kevin score for both games?

**2** There are 147 fish in a pond.
49 of them are black.
The rest are orange.
How many fish are orange?

**3** 98 boys sign up for a school camp.
154 girls sign up for the camp also.
How many children sign up for the camp in all?

**4** Jordan and Ling have 472 trading cards.
Ling has 178 trading cards.
How many trading cards does Jordan have?

**5** A bookstore has 179 chapter books.
It has 243 picture books.
How many chapter and picture books does the bookstore have?

**6** Lee has 528 United States and Singapore stamps.
He has 249 United States stamps.
How many Singapore stamps does he have?

ON YOUR OWN

**Go to Workbook A:**
**Practice 1, pages 73–76**

# 2 Adding On and Taking Away Sets

**Lesson Objectives**

- Model addition as joining sets.
- Model subtraction as taking away.
- Apply the inverse operations of addition and subtraction.

**Learn** **You can use bar models to show joining sets to add.**

Jenny has 87 marbles.
Her friend gives her 78 more marbles.
How many marbles does Jenny have now?

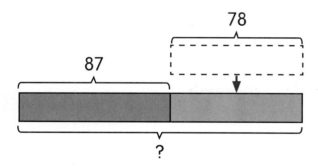

A set is a group of objects.

$87 + 78 = 165$

Jenny has 165 marbles now.

**Check!**

$165 - 78 = 87$
$165 - 87 = 78$

The answer is correct.

# Guided Practice

**Solve.**
**Use bar models to help you.**

**1** Carlos has 9 stickers.
His cousin gives him 3 stickers.
His sister buys him another 5 stickers.
How many stickers does Carlos have in all?

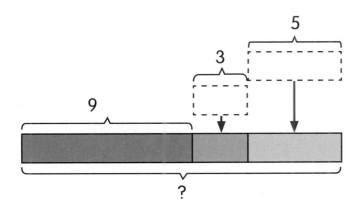

⬜ + ⬜ + ⬜ = ⬜

Carlos has ⬜ stickers in all.

## Check!

3 + 5 = 8

⬜ + 8 = ⬜

Is the answer correct?

# Hands-On Activity

 **STEP 1**

Your teacher will give you a bag. Put some small items in the bag. Take turns picking an item.

**STEP 2**

Think of a story using the item that you pick.

**STEP 3**

In your story, use the names of three friends and numbers less than 20.

 **STEP 4**

How many stories can you tell? Show each story with a bar model.

Here's a school story to get you started.

Greg has 8 crayons.
Tara gives him 9 more crayons.
Sam gives him another 5 crayons.
How many crayons does Greg have now?

**Learn** **You can use bar models to show taking away sets to subtract.**

A florist has 98 flowers.
She sells some of them.
She has 28 flowers left.
How many flowers does she sell?

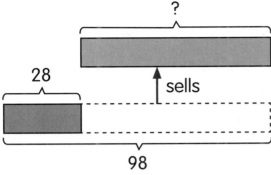

98 − 28 = 70

She sells 70 flowers.

Check!

70 + 28 = 98

The answer is correct.

## Guided Practice

**Solve.**
**Use the bar model to help you.**

2   Lena has 401 trading cards in her shop.
She sells 212 trading cards.
How many trading cards
does she have left?

Check!

[  ] + [  ] = [  ]

The answer is correct.

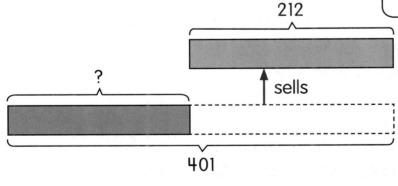

[  ] − [  ] = [  ]

She has [  ] trading cards left.

# READING AND WRITING MATH
## Math Journal

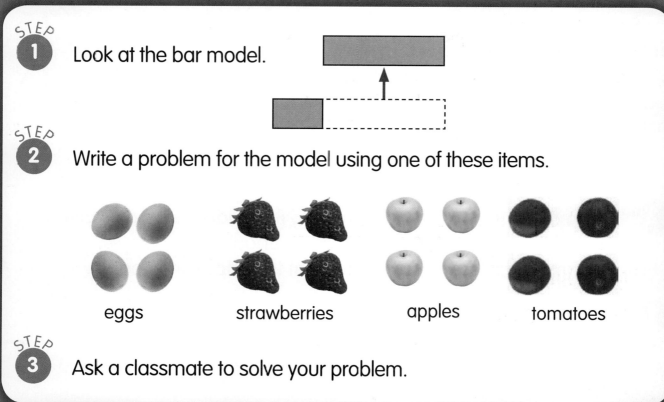

**STEP 1** Look at the bar model.

**STEP 2** Write a problem for the model using one of these items.

eggs          strawberries          apples          tomatoes

**STEP 3** Ask a classmate to solve your problem.

## Guided Practice

**Solve.**
**Use bar models to help you.**

**3** There are 625 children in the lunchroom.
56 more children come to the lunchroom.
How many children are in the lunchroom now?

**4** Sarah has 147 stickers.
Her friend gives her another 49 stickers.
How many stickers does she have altogether?

**5** A fruitstore owner has 742 apples to sell.
She sells 258 apples.
How many apples does she have left to sell?

## Let's Practice

**Solve.**
**Use bar models to help you.**

**1** The art teacher has 138 markers in a box.
She adds 55 markers to the box.
How many markers does she have in all?

**2** Adams Elementary School enrolled 785 children in September.
During the year, 156 children left the school.
How many children were enrolled at the end of the year?

**3** There are 88 people in a movie theater.
127 more people come into the theater.
How many people are in the theater now?

**4** There are 78 biscuits.
The baker bakes 159 more biscuits.
How many biscuits are there now?

**5** The library has 500 books.
248 books are checked out.
How many books does the library have now?

**6** Mr. Miller's toy store has 102 stuffed animals.
He sells 76 of them.
How many stuffed animals are there now?

ON YOUR OWN

Go to Workbook A:
Practice 2, pages 77–80

## LESSON 3 Comparing Two Sets

### Lesson Objectives

- Model addition and subtraction as comparing sets.
- Apply the inverse operations of addition and subtraction.

compare

**You can use bar models to show comparing sets to add.**

Keisha has 213 pins in her collection.
Fran has 78 more pins in her collection.
How many pins does Fran have in her collection?

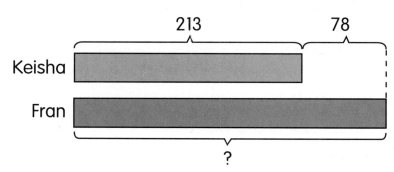

$213 + 78 = 291$

Fran has 291 pins in her collection.

**Check!**

$291 - 78 = 213$
$291 - 213 = 78$

The answer is correct.

# Guided Practice

**Solve.**
**Use the bar models to help you.**

**1** 305 children go to the zoo on Saturday.
278 more children go to the zoo on Sunday than on Saturday.
How many children go to the zoo on Sunday?

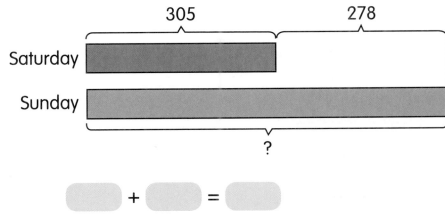

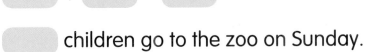

(  ) + (  ) = (  )

(  ) children go to the zoo on Sunday.

**Check!**

(  ) − (  ) = (  )

(  ) − (  ) = (  )

Is the answer correct?

**2** Sue has $55.
Hans has $12 more than Sue.
How much money does Hans have?

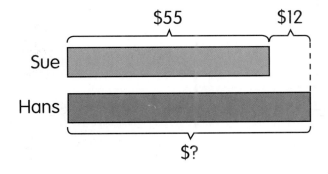

$ (  ) + $ (  ) = $ (  )

Hans has $ (  ).

**Check!**

(  ) − (  ) = (  )

(  ) − (  ) = (  )

Is the answer correct?

**Learn** You can use bar models to show comparing sets to subtract.

459 children were at the library yesterday.
46 fewer children are at the library today.
How many children are at the library today?

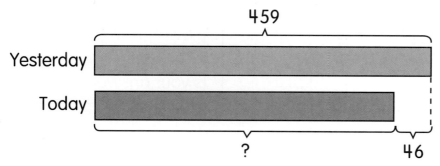

459 − 46 = 413

**Check!**

413 + 46 = 459

The answer is correct.

413 children are at the library today.

## Guided Practice

**Solve.**

**Use the bar models to help you.**

**Check!**

3   Rosa scores 824 points in a bowling contest.
Susan scores 157 points less than Rosa.
How many points does Susan score?

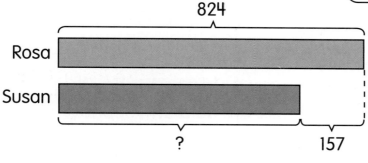

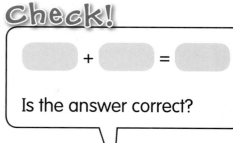

[____] + [____] = [____]

Is the answer correct?

[____] − [____] = [____]

Susan scores [____] points.

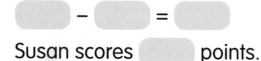

**4** In Store A, 300 video games are sold.
This is 126 more games sold than in Store B.
How many video games are sold in Store B?

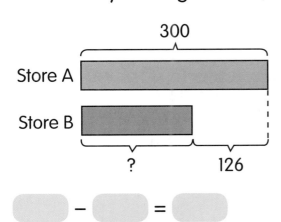

300

Store A

Store B

? 126

**Check!**

[ ] + [ ] = [ ]

Is your answer correct?

[ ] − [ ] = [ ]

[ ] video games are sold in Store B.

## Hands-On Activity

**WORK IN PAIRS**

**Ask your friend to draw a bar model for the first problem.
You will then choose + or − and solve the problem.
Reverse your roles for the second problem.**

**1** 95 cartons of milk are sold on Monday.
68 more cartons of milk are sold on Monday than on Tuesday.
How many cartons of milk are sold on Tuesday?

**2** Ben can put 150 photos into a photo album.
He can put 28 fewer photos into a scrapbook.
How many photos can Ben put into the scrapbook?

# Guided Practice

**Solve.**
**Choose + or − to solve the problems.**
**Draw bar models to help you.**

**5** Mika uses 56 beads to make a bracelet.
Emma uses 9 fewer beads than Mika.
How many beads does Emma use?

**6** There are 305 girls at the high school play.
There are 48 fewer boys than girls.
How many boys are at the play?

**7** A fruit seller has 140 strawberries.
He has 29 fewer pears than strawberries.
How many pears does he have?

**8** Pepe spends $78 on clothing.
He spends $49 less than John.
How much does John spend?

**9** Uncle Denzel and Uncle Mark work at a coffee shop.
Uncle Denzel works 210 hours.
Uncle Denzel works 34 fewer hours than Uncle Mark.
How many hours does Uncle Mark work?

**10** There are 78 chickens at a farm.
There are 39 more geese than chickens.
How many geese are there?

# Let's Practice

**Solve.**
**Use bar models to help you.**

**1** The length of Pole A is 36 feet.
Pole B is 9 feet shorter than Pole A.
How long is Pole B?

**2** Lucy uses 64 inches of ribbon.
She uses 37 inches less than Wendy.
How many inches of ribbon does Wendy use?

**3** Carlos sells 478 tickets for the school fair.
Marissa sells 129 more tickets than Carlos.
How many tickets does Marissa sell?

**4** A red box has 326 pencils.
The red box has 78 fewer pencils than the blue box.
How many pencils are in the blue box?

**5** There are 586 red counters.
There are 137 fewer white counters than red counters.
How many white counters are there?

**6** Julian drives 259 miles in one day.
He drives 109 more miles than Larry.
How many miles does Larry drive?

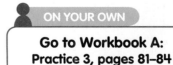

ON YOUR OWN

Go to Workbook A:
Practice 3, pages 81–84

# Real-World Problems: Two-Step Problems

**LESSON 4**

## Lesson Objectives

- Use bar models to solve two-step addition and subtraction problems.
- Apply the inverse operations of addition and subtraction.

*Learn* **You can use bar models to solve two-step problems.**

There are 26 boys and 19 girls in a class.
Later, 7 children leave the class.
How many children are in the class at first?
How many children are in the class now?

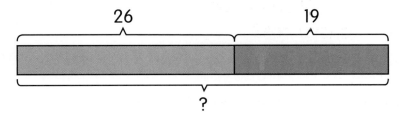

$26 + 19 = 45$
There are 45 children in the class at first.

**Check!**
$45 - 19 = 26$
$45 - 26 = 19$

The answer is correct.

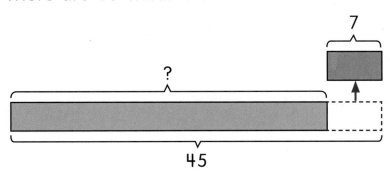

$45 - 7 = 38$
There are 38 children in the class now.

**Check!**
$38 + 7 = 45$

The answer is correct.

# Guided Practice

**Solve.**
**Use the bar models to help you.**

**1** Mr. Castro drives 341 miles.
Mrs. Castro drives 279 miles more than Mr. Castro.

    **a** How far does Mrs. Castro drive?

    **b** How far do Mr. and Mrs. Castro drive altogether?

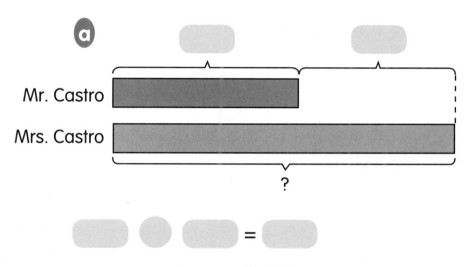

Mrs. Castro drives ____ miles.

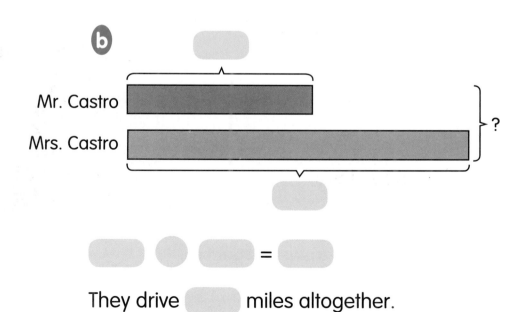

They drive ____ miles altogether.

**2** There are 22 boys and 16 girls in Vicky's class.
There are 5 more children in Joshua's class than in Vicky's class.

**a** How many children are in Vicky's class?

**b** How many children are in Joshua's class?

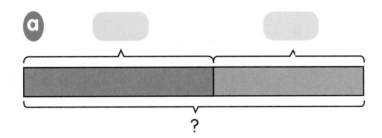

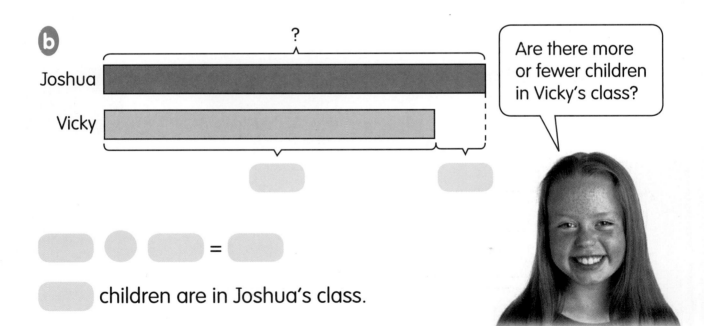

children are in Vicky's class.

children are in Joshua's class.

Are there more or fewer children in Vicky's class?

**3** Anya has 264 United States and Mexican stamps in all.
93 stamps are Mexican stamps.

**ⓐ** How many United States stamps does Anya have?

**ⓑ** How many more United States stamps than Mexican stamps
does Anya have?

**ⓐ**

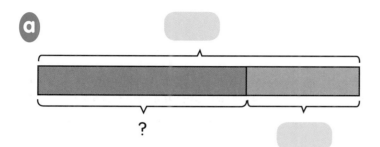

Anya has ⬭ United States stamps.

Do I add or subtract?

**ⓑ**

United States stamps

Mexican stamps

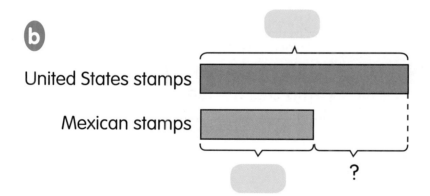

Anya has ⬭ more United States stamps than Mexican stamps.

**4** Barry has 345 marbles.
He gives Andy 78 marbles.
Now, Barry has 183 blue marbles and some red marbles.
How many red marbles does Barry have now?

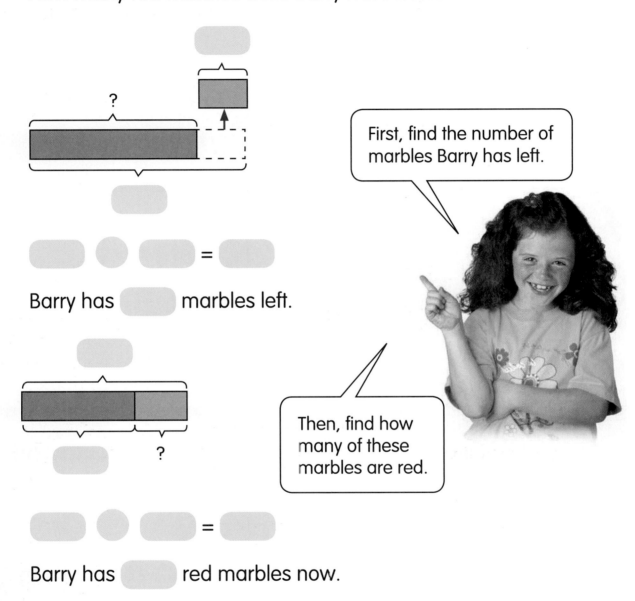

Barry has ▢ marbles left.

▢ ● ▢ = ▢

Barry has ▢ red marbles now.

First, find the number of marbles Barry has left.

Then, find how many of these marbles are red.

## Solve.
## Draw bar models to help you.

**5** Tara and Jason collect stamps.
Tara has 165 stamps.
She has 48 more stamps than Jason.
How many stamps do they have altogether? ▢

**Solve.**
**Draw bar models to help you.**

**6** A tall bookcase has 56 math books and 78 reading books.
A short bookcase has 39 fewer books.
How many books are in the short bookcase? ⬭

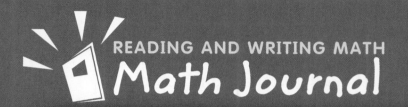

READING AND WRITING MATH
**Math Journal**

| Kelly | 327 | sells | stickers | Rashid |
| 753 | stamps | Sal | in all | how many |
| left | Kevin | 468 | buys | buttons |

**Use the words and numbers above to write:**

**1** two real-world addition problems.

**2** two real-world subtraction problems.

## Let's Practice

**Solve.**
**Draw bar models to help you.**

**1** The paper store receives 528 newspapers in a week.
Ms. Diaz delivers 274 newspapers to local homes.
Mr. Miguel sells all except 56 of the remaining papers.

**a** How many newspapers are not delivered?

**b** How many of these does Mr. Miguel sell?

**2** The pet store has 420 goldfish for sale.
It has 88 more guppies than goldfish.
Tomorrow it will get 55 more guppies.
How many guppies will the pet store have then?

**3** An electronics store has 750 computers and television sets.
429 are computers.
The store sells 86 television sets.
How many television sets are not sold?

**4** Pam uses 328 seashells in a craft project.
Sharon uses 85 more seashells than Pam for her project.
How many seashells do they use altogether?

**5** Tom has 275 comic books in his collection.
Chris sells 82 comic books to Tom.
Then Chris has 148 comic books left.
How many more comic books does Tom
have than Chris now?

ON YOUR OWN

**Go to Workbook A:**
**Practice 4, pages 85–92**

## CRITICAL THINKING SKILLS
# Put On Your Thinking Cap!

**PROBLEM SOLVING**
Kathy has 18 more video games than Lisa.
Kathy gives Lisa some video games.
Then they both have the same number of games.
How many video games does Kathy give
to Lisa?

Draw **bar models**
to help you.

ON YOUR OWN

**Go to Workbook A:**
**Put on Your Thinking Cap!**
**pages 93–94**

# Chapter Wrap Up

**You have learned...**

## Using Bar Models: Addition and Subtraction

Solve using addition and subtraction.

**1**

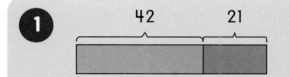

42          21

How many marbles are there?

$42 + 21 = 63$

There are 63 marbles.

Check the answer.

$63 - 21 = 42$

$63 - 42 = 21$

The answer is correct.

**2**

How many marbles?

78

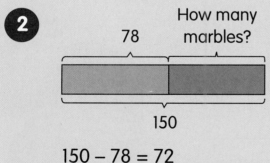

150

$150 - 78 = 72$

There are 72 marbles.

Check the answer.

$72 + 78 = 150$

The answer is correct.

**3**

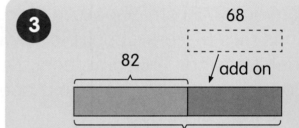

68

82          add on

How many marbles are there in all?

$82 + 68 = 150$

There are 150 marbles in all.

Check the answer.

**4**

How many marbles are left?

53

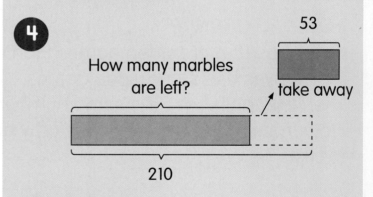

take away

210

$210 - 53 = 157$

There are 157 marbles left.

Check the answer.

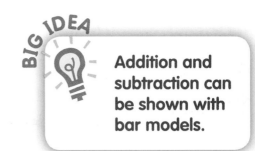

Draw bar models for one-step addition and subtraction problems.

Draw bar models for two-step addition and subtraction problems.

**5**

400    203 more

Boy A

Boy B

How many marbles are there?

400 + 203 = 603
Boy B has 603 marbles.
Check the answer.

**6**

How many marbles are there?    132 fewer

Girl A

Girl B

263

263 − 132 = 131
Girl A has 131 marbles.
Check the answer.

**7**

How many marbles fewer?

89

Boy A

Boy B

?

136

**a**  136 − 89 = 47
Boy A has 47 fewer marbles than Boy B.

**b**  89 + 136 = 225
They have 225 marbles in all.
Check the answer.

ON YOUR OWN

**Go to Workbook A:**
**Chapter Review/Test,**
**pages 95–98**

# Multiplication and Division

I am having guests for lunch. How much of each do I need for the 8 of us?

**Salad** (Serves 4)

What you need
6 cups   shredded lettuce
3 cups   sliced carrots
2 cups   sliced tomato
1 cup    sunflower seeds
1 cup    salad dressing

BIG IDEA

Multiplication and division use equal groups.

# Recall Prior Knowledge

## Adding equal groups

$2 + 2 + 2 + 2 = 8$

4 groups of 2 = 8

4 twos = 8

## Sharing equally

Share 10 marbles equally among 5 children.

 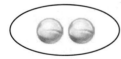   

Each child gets 2 marbles.

## Grouping

Put 15 oranges into groups of 3.

There are 5 groups of oranges.

**Find the missing numbers.**

1

⬭ groups of ⬭ = ⬭

2  4 threes = ⬭ + ⬭ + ⬭ + ⬭ = ⬭

3  5 fours = ⬭ groups of ⬭ = ⬭

**Find the set that does not belong.**

4  | 14 | | 4 + 7 + 4 + 7 | | 2 groups of 7 | | 7 + 7 |

5  | 8 + 8 + 8 + 8 + 8 | | 5 groups of 8 | | 8 + 5 | | 5 eights |

**Find the missing numbers.**

6  Put 9 apples into 3 bags.

There are ⬭ apples in each bag.

7  Put 8 muffins in groups of 2.

There are ⬭ groups of muffins.

# LESSON 1 How to Multiply

## Lesson Objectives

- Use equal groups and repeated addition to multiply.
- Make multiplication stories about pictures.
- Make multiplication sentences.

**Vocabulary**

| | |
|---|---|
| times | repeated addition |
| equal | multiplication sentence |
| group | multiplication stories |
| multiply | |

**Learn** **You can multiply when you have equal groups.**

How many horses are there?

There are two ways to find the number of horses.

First, count the number of equal groups.
There are 3 groups.
Then, count the number of horses in each **group**.

There are 5 horses in each group.
Use **repeated addition** or **multiply**
to find the number of horses.

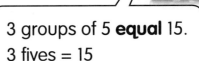

3 groups of 5 **equal** 15.
3 fives = 15

$5 + 5 + 5 = 15$
$3 \times 5 = 15$

× is read as **times**.
It means to **multiply,** or to put all the equal groups together.

There are 15 horses in all.
$3 \times 5 = 15$ is a **multiplication sentence**.
You read it as **three times five is equal to fifteen**.

Continued on next page

**Or**

First, count the number of items in each group.
There are 5 horses in each group.
Then, count the number of groups.

There are 3 groups.
The number 5 multiplies 3 times.

$5 \times 3 = 5 + 5 + 5 = 15$

There are 15 horses in all.

5 **times** 3 is equal to 15.

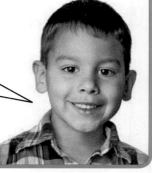

## Guided Practice

**Find the missing numbers.**

**1**

How many plates are there?

How many muffins are on each plate?

How many muffins are there in all?

$3 \times$ ⬚ $=$ ⬚ or $2 \times$ ⬚ $=$ ⬚

There are ⬚ muffins in all.

**Find the missing numbers.**

**1** How many chairs are there?

4 + 4 = ⬚

2 × 4 = ⬚

**2** How many crayons are there?

7 + 7 = ⬚

2 × ⬚ = ⬚

**3** How many beads are there?

⬚ + ⬚ + ⬚ + ⬚ + ⬚ = ⬚

⬚ × ⬚ = ⬚

**ON YOUR OWN**

**Go to Workbook A:**
**Practice 1, pages 107–108**

**Learn** **You can make multiplication stories.**

There are 5 groups of socks.

Each group has 2 socks.

$2 + 2 + 2 + 2 + 2 = 10$

5 groups of $2 = 10$

$5 \times 2 = 10$

There are 10 socks.

## Guided Practice

**Tell a multiplication story about these baby turtles.**

2   There are ⬜ groups of turtles.

Each group has ⬜ turtles.

⬜ × ⬜ = ⬜

There are ⬜ turtles.

**Tell multiplication stories.**
**Then write the multiplication sentences.**

3  ⬜

4  ⬜

# Let's Explore!

Amy puts her toys into 5 groups in this way.

She is trying to write a multiplication sentence.
Can she do it?
Explain why.

Put the toys in groups in different ways.
Write a multiplication sentence for each way.
What do you notice?

To write a multiplication sentence, the groups must be equal.

## Which of these sentences are correct?

**1** 5 × 2 has the same answer as 52.

**2** The picture shows 4 × 4.

**3** 8 × 3 = 3 + 3 + 3 + 3 + 3 + 3 + 3 + 3

**4** 2 × 6 = 6 + 6 + 6 + 6 + 6 + 6

**5** 4 × 7 = 7 + 7 + 7 + 7

**6** Think of some numbers less than 13.
Make multiplication sentences with your numbers.

# Let's Practice

**Look at the picture.**

**Make some multiplication stories about:**

**1** balloons

**2** sandwiches

**3** drinks

**Example**
5 children have 2 hats each.
There are 10 hats altogether.

ON YOUR OWN

Go to Workbook A:
Practice 2, pages 109–110

# LESSON 2 How to Divide

**Lesson Objectives**

• Divide to share equally.

• Divide by repeated subtraction of equal groups.

**Vocabulary**

share     division sentences

divide     repeated subtraction

equal groups

**Learn** **You divide when you share equally.**

David has 6 apples.
He wants to **divide** the apples into 2 **equal groups**.
How many apples are there in each group?

$6 \div 2 = 3$

÷ is read as **divided by**, and stands for **division**.

Read $6 \div 2 = 3$ as **six divided by two is equal to three**.
There are 3 apples in each group.

Now David wants to divide the 6 apples into 3 equal groups.
How many apples are there in each group?

$6 \div 3 = 2$

How do I read $6 \div 3 = 2$?

There are 2 apples in each group.

$6 \div 2 = 3$ and $6 \div 3 = 2$ are **division sentences**.

# Guided Practice

**Solve.**

**1**   Al takes 15 dog biscuits from a tin.
He gives an equal number of biscuits to each of his 3 dogs.
How many biscuits does each dog get?

$15 \div 3 =$ 

Each dog gets      biscuits.


**2**   Then Al takes another 15 dog biscuits from the tin.
He gives an equal number of biscuits to each of his 5 puppies.
How many biscuits does each puppy get?

$15 \div$     $=$ 

Each puppy gets     biscuits.

**You can divide by using repeated subtraction of equal groups.**

Wendy has 6 marbles.
She wants to give 2 marbles to each of her friends.
How many friends get marbles from her?

First, she gives 2 marbles to Pete.
How many marbles does she have left?

$6 - 2 = 4$
She has 4 marbles left.

Then, she gives 2 marbles to Shantel.
How many marbles does she have left?

$4 - 2 = 2$
She has 2 marbles left.

Finally, she gives 2 marbles to Teddy.
How many marbles does she have left?

$2 - 2 = 0$
She has 0 marbles left.

Subtract 2 until you get 0.
How many times do you subtract 2?

3 times!

Wendy divides her 6 marbles equally by giving
2 marbles to each friend.
So, **3** friends get marbles from her.

$6 \underbrace{- 2 - 2 - 2} = 0$ is the same as $6 \div 2 = \mathbf{3}$

groups of 2 are
subtracted **3** times

Because you are subtracting 2 repeatedly,
this is **repeated subtraction.**

**Learn** **You can record repeated subtraction
in a number sentence.**

$8 \div 2 = ?$

**Step 1**
Subtract groups of 2 until you have 0.

**Step 2**
Count the number of times you subtract the groups of 2.

**Step 3**
The number of times is the answer.

$$8 \overbrace{- 2 - 2 - 2 - 2}^{\text{4 times}} = 0$$

So, $8 \div 2 = 4$.

# Guided Practice

**Solve.**

**Use repeated subtraction to divide.**

**3** Jared has 12 basketball cards.
He divides the cards equally among his friends.
Each friend gets 4 cards.
How many friends are there?

$12 - \boxed{\phantom{00}} - \boxed{\phantom{00}} - \boxed{\phantom{00}} = 0$

Subtract groups of four $\boxed{\phantom{00}}$ times.

$12 \div 4 = \boxed{\phantom{00}}$

There are $\boxed{\phantom{00}}$ friends.

**4** Karen has 18 basketball cards.
She gives the cards to some friends.
If each friend gets 3 cards, how many friends are there?

$18 - \boxed{\phantom{00}} - \boxed{\phantom{00}} - \boxed{\phantom{00}} - \boxed{\phantom{00}} - \boxed{\phantom{00}} - \boxed{\phantom{00}} = 0$

$18 \div 3 = \boxed{\phantom{00}}$

There are $\boxed{\phantom{00}}$ friends.

 **Hands-On Activity**

## Use 24 counters.

**1** Divide the counters into equal groups of 2.

Write a division sentence to show how many groups there are.

**2** Using all the counters, make equal groups of:

**ⓐ** 3     **ⓑ** 4     **ⓒ** 6     **ⓓ** 8     **ⓔ** 12

For each, write a division sentence to show how many groups there are.

## Use 20 craft sticks.

**3** Make as many of these shapes as possible.

**ⓐ**           **ⓑ**

Write a division sentence to show how many of each shape there are.

## Use 18 craft sticks.

**4** Make as many of these shapes as possible.

**ⓐ**           **ⓑ**

Write a division sentence to show how many of each shape there are.

# Let's Practice

**Find the missing numbers.**

**1** Divide 8 robots into 4 equal groups.

8 ÷ ⬚ = ⬚

There are ⬚ robots in each group.

**2** Divide 27 eggs equally into 3 baskets.

27 ÷ ⬚ = ⬚

There are ⬚ eggs in each basket.

**3** Divide 40 pancakes onto plates with 10 on each plate.

40 ÷ ⬚ = ⬚

There are ⬚ plates of 10 pancakes.

**4** Divide 14 pencils into bundles of 2.

14 ÷ ⬚ = ⬚

There are ⬚ bundles of pencils.

## Use repeated subtraction to find the missing numbers.

**Example**

20 ÷ 4 = 5

20 − 4 − 4 − 4 − 4 − 4 = 0

Subtract groups of four 5 times.

**5** 12 ÷ 3 = ⬚

12 − ⬚ − ⬚ − ⬚ − ⬚ = 0

Subtract groups of three ⬚ times.

**6** 18 ÷ 6 = ⬚

18 − ⬚ − ⬚ − ⬚ = 0

Subtract groups of six ⬚ times.

ON YOUR OWN

**Go to Workbook A:**
**Practice 3, pages 111–114**

# LESSON 3 Real-World Problems: Multiplication and Division

**Lesson Objectives**

- Solve multiplication word problems.
- Solve division word problems.

**Learn** **Read, understand, and solve this word problem.**

There are 3 children.
The teacher gives each child 6 seashells.
How many seashells does the teacher give out?

$3 \times 6 = 18$
The teacher gives out 18 seashells.

## Guided Practice

**Solve.**

  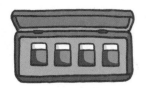

Sandra has 2 pencil cases.
There are 4 erasers in each pencil case.
How many erasers does Sandra have?

Sandra has ⬜ erasers.

**Read, understand, and solve this word problem.**

Mrs. Carter has 12 markers.
She divides them equally among 6 children.
How many markers does each child get?

$12 \div 6 = 2$

Each child gets 2 markers.

## Guided Practice

**Solve.**

A clown has 18 balloons.
He gives an equal number to 9 children.
How many balloons does each child get?

[    ] ÷ [    ] = [    ]

Each child gets [    ] balloons.

**Read, understand, and solve this word problem.**

Some children collect 24 shells.
Each child gets 4 shells.
How many children are there altogether?

$24 \div 4 = 6$

There are 6 children altogether.

## Guided Practice

**Solve.**

**3**

Mrs. Walsh bakes 16 vegetable pies.
She wants to put 8 vegetable pies in each box.
How many boxes does she need?

[    ] ÷ [    ] = [    ]

She needs [    ] boxes.

# Let's Practice

**Write a multiplication or division sentence for each problem.**
**Then solve.**

**1** Juan has 3 jars.
He puts 6 almonds into each jar.
How many almonds does Juan have?

**2** Mr. Wallace gives 7 books to each of his 2 sons.
How many books does he give to his sons?

**3** Melanie has 3 cups.
She puts 5 marbles in each cup.
How many marbles are in the cups?

**4** Mr. Smith put 15 flower pots in 3 rows.
He put the same number of flower pots in each row.
How many flower pots are in each row?

**5** Clara saves $2 a day.
How many days will she take to save $14?

**6** Mr. Kent has 24 stickers.
He gives Jason 6 stickers each time Jason finishes reading a book.
How many books must Jason read to get all 24 stickers?

**ON YOUR OWN**

**Go to Workbook A:**
**Practice 4, pages 115–118**

## Let's Explore!

Two types of animals are playing.
Some of the animals have 2 legs.
The others have 4 legs.
The animals have 10 legs altogether.

How many animals of each type are there?

**Draw diagrams** to help you.
You can have more than one
correct answer.

## CRITICAL THINKING SKILLS
## Put On Your Thinking Cap!

**PROBLEM SOLVING**

Zita opens her birthday present.
She finds a big box.
The big box has 4 identical medium boxes.
Each medium box has 6 identical small boxes.
How many small boxes are there in the big box in all?

**ON YOUR OWN**

Go to Workbook A:
Put on Your Thinking Cap!
pages 119–120

# Chapter Wrap Up

**You have learned...**

to use repeated addition or multiply to find the total number of things in equal groups.

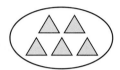 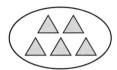 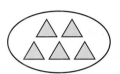

There are 3 groups.
There are 5 △ in each group.
$5 + 5 + 5 = 15$
$3 \times 5 = 15$

There are 5 △ in each group.
There are 3 groups.
$5 \times 3 = 5 + 5 + 5$
$\qquad = 15$

to divide a given number of objects equally to find:
- the number of things in each group.

Divide 12 things into 3 equal groups.

$12 \div 3 = 4$

There are 4 things in each group.

- the number of groups.

Divide 12 things so there are 4 things in each group.

$12 \div 4 = 3$

There are 3 groups.

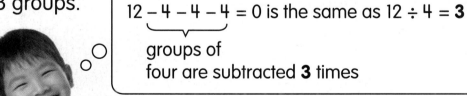

$12 - 4 - 4 - 4 = 0$ is the same as $12 \div 4 = \mathbf{3}$

groups of
four are subtracted **3** times

to solve real-world problems with multiplication and division.

**ON YOUR OWN**

Go to Workbook A:
**Chapter Review/Test,
pages 121–126**

# Multiplication Tables of 2, 5, and 10

2 toy soldiers marching in a line
2 toy soldiers marching in a line
If 2 more soldiers join them in the line,
There will be 4 toy soldiers marching in a line.

4 toy soldiers marching in a line
4 toy soldiers marching in a line
If 2 more soldiers join them in the line,
There will be 6 toy soldiers marching in a line.

6 toy soldiers marching in a line
6 toy soldiers marching in a line
If 2 more soldiers join them in the line,
There will be 8 toy soldiers marching in a line.

**BIG IDEA**

Known multiplication facts can be used to find other multiplication and division facts.

# Recall Prior Knowledge

## Number patterns

**1** 2, 4, 6, 8, 10, 12, 14, 16, 18, 20

**2** 5, 10, 15, 20, 25, 30, 35, 40, 45, 50

**3** 10, 20, 30, 40, 50, 60, 70, 80, 90, 100

## Using equal groups to multiply

5 groups of 2 = 10
2 + 2 + 2 + 2 + 2 = 10
5 twos = 10
5 × 2 = 10

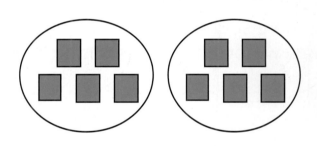

2 groups of 5 = 10
5 + 5 = 10
2 fives = 10
2 × 5 = 10

**Find the missing numbers in each number pattern.**

**1** 2, 4, 6, 8, 10, ____, ____, ____, ____

**2** 5, 10, 15, ____, ____, ____, ____, 40

**3** 100, 90, ____, ____, ____, ____, 40, 30

**Find the missing numbers.**

**4**

____ twos = ____ groups of ____

**5**

____ fives = ____ groups of ____

# Find the missing numbers.

**6**

**7**

# 1 Multiplying 2: Skip-counting

**Lesson Objectives**

- Skip-count by 2s.
- Solve multiplication word problems.

**Vocabulary**
skip-count

**Learn** **You can skip-count by 2s to find how many there are.**

There are 2 scooters in 1 group.

$1 \times 2 = 2$

How many scooters are in 10 groups?

1 group of 2 scooters

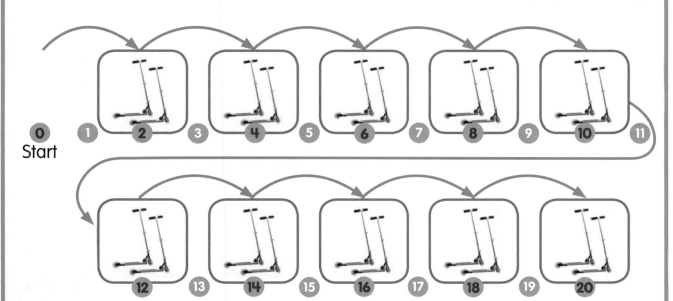

**2, 4, 6, 8, 10, 12, 14, 16, 18, 20**

$10 \times 2 = 20$

There are 20 scooters.

I count by 2s.

Continued on next page

Ali has 7 bags.
There are 2 pineapples in each bag.
How many pineapples does he have altogether?

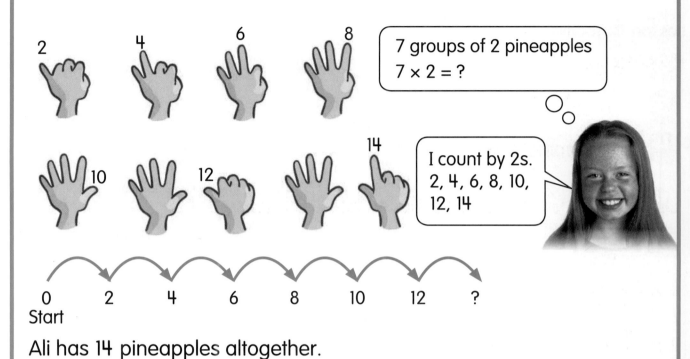

7 groups of 2 pineapples

$7 \times 2 = ?$

I count by 2s.
2, 4, 6, 8, 10,
12, 14

0   2   4   6   8   10   12   ?
Start

Ali has 14 pineapples altogether.

## Guided Practice

**Use skip-counting to find the missing numbers.**

1   There are 8 fish bowls.
2 guppies are in each bowl.
How many guppies are there
in all?

8 groups of
2 guppies

I count by 2s.
2, ___, ___, ___,
___, ___, ___, ___

 × ___ = ___

There are ___ guppies in all.

# Let's Practice

**Find the missing numbers.**

**1**  2 groups of 2 = ⬚ × 2

**2**  6 groups of 2 = ⬚ × 2

**3**  1 group of 2 = ⬚ × 2

**4**  9 groups of 2 = ⬚ × 2

**Use skip-counting to find the missing numbers.**

Example

$4 \times 2 = ?$

$4 \times 2 = 8$

```
   0   2   4   6   8
 Start
```

**5**  $3 \times 2 = $ ⬚

**6**  $10 \times 2 = $ ⬚

**Multiply by 2 to find the missing numbers.**

**7**  $7 \times 2 = $ ⬚

**8**  $5 \times 2 = $ ⬚

**9**  $6 \times 2 = $ ⬚

**10**  $8 \times 2 = $ ⬚

**Solve.**

**11**  There are 9 girls.
Each girl wears 2 hairclips in her hair.
How many hairclips are there in all?

**12**  Karan and Jose eat 2 tacos each for lunch.
How many tacos do they eat in all?

ON YOUR OWN

Go to Workbook A:
Practice 1, pages 127–128

# LESSON 2

# Multiplying 2: Using Dot Paper

## Lesson Objectives

- Use dot paper to multiply by 2.
- Use known multiplication facts to find new multiplication facts.
- Identify related multiplication facts.
- Solve multiplication word problems.

**Vocabulary**
dot paper
related multiplication facts

**Learn You can use dot paper to multiply by 2.**

lambs

Each sheep has 2 lambs.

How many lambs do the 3 sheep have in all?

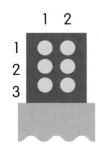

This is **dot paper**. It shows 3 rows of 2.

$3 \times 2 = 6$

3 sheep have 6 lambs in all.

# Guided Practice

## Use dot paper to find the missing numbers.

**1** Sam has 4 bundles of pencils.
Each bundle has 2 pencils.
How many pencils does he have in all?

$4 \times 2 = $ ▢

Sam has ▢ pencils in all.

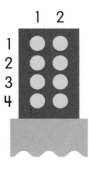

**2** There are 5 pairs of socks on a clothes line.
How many socks are on the clothes line?

$5 \times 2 = $ ▢

▢ socks are on the clothes line.

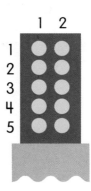

**Learn** **You can use multiplication facts you know to find other multiplication facts.**

$6 \times 2 = ?$

Start with 5 groups of 2.

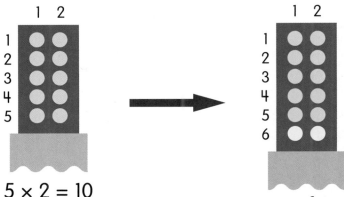

$5 \times 2 = 10$

$6 \times 2 = $ 5 groups of 2 + 1 group of 2
$= 10 + 2$
$= 12$

6 × 2 is the same as adding 1 group of 2 to 5 × 2.

## Guided Practice

**Use facts you know to find the missing numbers.**

**3**  $7 \times 2 = ?$

Start with 5 groups of 2.

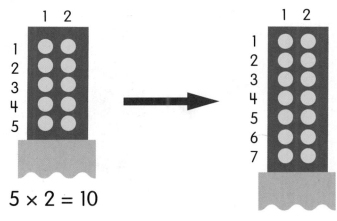

$5 \times 2 = 10$

7 × 2 is the same as adding ⬜ groups of 2 to 5 × 2.

$7 \times 2 = $ 5 groups of 2 + ⬜ groups of 2
$= 10 + $ ⬜
$= $ ⬜

**You can use multiplication facts you know to find other multiplication facts.**

$9 \times 2 = ?$

Start with 10 groups of 2.

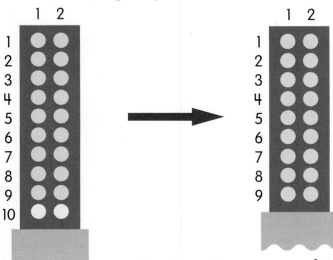

$10 \times 2 = 20$

9 × 2 is the same as subtracting 1 group of 2 from 10 × 2.

$9 \times 2 = $ 10 groups of 2 − 1 group of 2
$= 20 - 2$
$= 18$

## Guided Practice

**Use facts you know to find the missing numbers.**

**4**  $8 \times 2 = ?$
Start with 10 groups of 2.

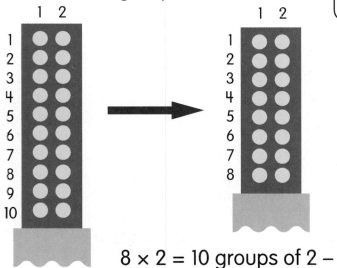

$10 \times 2 = 20$

8 × 2 is the same as subtracting ____ groups of 2 from 10 × 2.

$8 \times 2 = $ 10 groups of 2 − ____ groups of 2
$= 20 - $ ____
$= $ ____

## Multiplication Table of 2

| | | | | |
|---|---|---|---|---|
| 1 | × | 2 | = | 2 |
| 2 | × | 2 | = | 4 |
| 3 | × | 2 | = | 6 |
| 4 | × | 2 | = | 8 |
| 5 | × | 2 | = | 10 |
| 6 | × | 2 | = | 12 |
| 7 | × | 2 | = | 14 |
| 8 | × | 2 | = | 16 |
| 9 | × | 2 | = | 18 |
| 10 | × | 2 | = | 20 |

**Learn** **You can multiply numbers in any order.**

$4 \times 2 = 8$          $2 \times 4 = 8$

$4 \times 2 = 2 \times 4$
These are **related multiplication facts**.

## Guided Practice

**Use dot paper to find the missing numbers.**

5      ▢ × ▢ = 12          ▢ × ▢ = 12

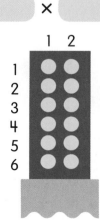

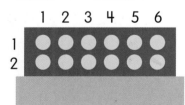

**160**  **Chapter 6**  Multiplication Tables of 2, 5, and 10

# Let's Practice

**Find the missing numbers.**

**1**  $5 \times 2 =$ ▢    $6 \times 2 =$ ▢ $+ 2 =$ ▢

  $7 \times 2 =$ ▢ $+ 4 =$ ▢

**2**  $10 \times 2 =$ ▢    $9 \times 2 =$ ▢ $- 2 =$ ▢

  $8 \times 2 =$ ▢ $- 4 =$ ▢

**Use dot paper to find the missing numbers.**

**3**  $3 \times 2 =$ ▢       **4**  $7 \times 2 =$ ▢

  $2 \times 3 =$ ▢         $2 \times 7 =$ ▢

**5**  $8 \times 2 =$ ▢       **6**  $9 \times 2 =$ ▢

  $2 \times 8 =$ ▢         $2 \times 9 =$ ▢

**7**  Andre, Brad, Cedric and Deon have 2 baseball caps each.
  How many baseball caps do they have in all?

**8**  There are 6 pairs of shoes on a shelf.
  How many shoes are there in all?

ON YOUR OWN

**Go to Workbook A:**
**Practice 2, pages 129–132**

# LESSON 3 Multiplying 5: Skip-counting

**Lesson Objectives**

- Skip-count by 5s.
- Solve multiplication word problems.

**WORKING TOGETHER  Game**

## Skip Fives!

Players: 4–6
You need:
- one hundreds chart
- counters
- number cube

**STEP 1**  Each player chooses a color and gets 10 counters of that color.

**STEP 2**  Player 1 rolls the number cube.
If a 5 is rolled, the player counts 5.
Then the player calls out
the number.
The other players check
the answer.
If the answer is correct,
Player 1 places a counter
over the number.

5

Correct

**3** Players who do not roll
a 5 lose a turn.
Players who do roll a 5, count on
from the last counter.
Take turns to play.

You lose
a turn.

STEP

**4** After a counter is placed over
the number 100, count the number
of counters of each color.
The player with the most
counters on the hundreds
chart wins.
Do not remove the counters.
What pattern do you see on
the hundreds chart?

## Guided Practice

**Continue each skip-counting pattern.**
**Use a hundreds chart to help you.**

**1** 15, 20, _____ , _____ , 35, 40, _____ , _____ , 55, _____

**2** _____ , 60, _____ , 70, 75, _____ , _____ , 90, 95, _____

**3** 45, _____ , _____ , 30, 25, _____ , _____ , 10, _____

## You can skip-count by 5s to find how many there are.

1 finger stands for 1 group of 5.

$1 \times 5 = 5$

1 finger stands for 5.

Skip-count by 5s with your fingers!

5

What do the 10 fingers stand for?

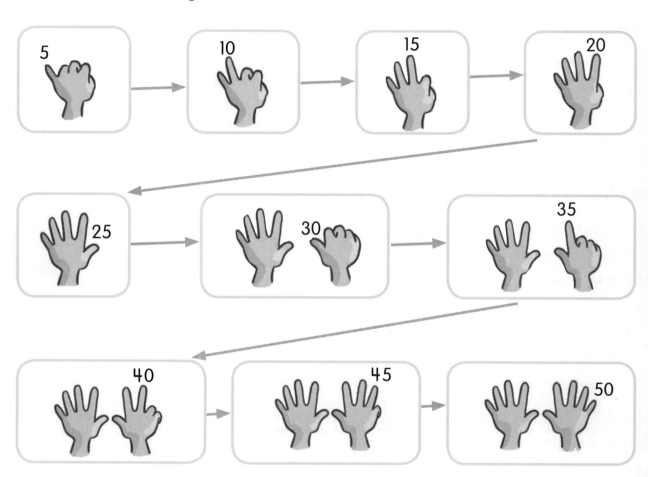

$10 \times 5 = 50$

The 10 fingers stand for 50.

Nita has 7 bunches of flowers.
Each bunch has 5 flowers.
How many flowers does she have in all?

$7 \times 5 = ?$

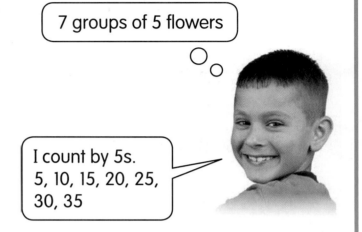

7 groups of 5 flowers

Nita has 35 flowers in all.

I count by 5s.
5, 10, 15, 20, 25,
30, 35

## Guided Practice

**Use skip-counting to find the missing numbers.**

**4** Dean has 6 starfish in his tank.
Each starfish has 5 arms.
How many arms do the 6 starfish have in all?

6 groups of 5 arms

I count by 5s.
5, 10, [    ], [    ],
[    ], [    ]

[    ] × [    ] = [    ]

They have [    ] arms in all.

# Coin and Number Cube Game

Players: 4–6
You need:
- worksheets
- a number cube
- a coin
- stickers
- number cards from 1 to 10

**STEP 1** Write these numbers on the stickers.
Paste them on the two sides of the coin.

**STEP 2** Put the number cards in a stack.

**STEP 3** Each player uses a worksheet.

| x | 1 | 2 | 3 | 4 | 5 | 6 | 7 | 8 | 9 | 10 |
|---|---|---|---|---|---|---|---|---|---|----|
| 2 | | | | | | | | | | |
| 5 | | | | | | | | | | |

**STEP 4** Player 1 tosses the coin and draws a number card.

**STEP 5** Player 1 multiplies the two numbers and writes the answer on the worksheet.

**STEP 6** The other players check the answer.
Players take turns.

The first player to fill 10 boxes on the worksheet wins!

# Let's Practice

**Find the missing numbers.**

**1**  2 groups of 5 = [    ] × 5

**2**  5 groups of 5 = [    ] × 5

**3**  6 groups of 5 = [    ] × 5

**4**  8 groups of 5 = [    ] × 5

**Use skip-counting to find the missing numbers.**

 5   10   15   20   25  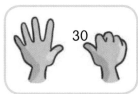 30  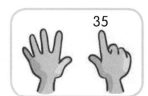 35

**5**  5 × 5 = [    ]

**6**  7 × 5 = [    ]

**Multiply by 5 to find the missing numbers.**

**7**  3 × 5 = [    ]

**8**  6 × 5 = [    ]

**9**  9 × 5 = [    ]

**10**  4 × 5 = [    ]

**Solve.**

**11**  Megan has 5 bags.
She puts 5 apples in each bag.
How many apples does she have in the bags?

**12**  Mr. Lee sells 5 pencils in a box.
He sells 8 boxes of pencils.
How many pencils does he sell?

**13**  A farmer has 5 chickens in each coop.
She has 6 coops.
How many chickens does she have in all?

ON YOUR OWN

Go to Workbook A:
Practice 3, pages 133–136

# LESSON
# 4 Multiplying 5: Using Dot Paper

**Lesson Objectives**

- Use dot paper to multiply by 5.
- Use known multiplication facts to find new multiplication facts.
- Identify related multiplication facts.
- Solve multiplication word problems.

**Learn** **You can use dot paper to multiply by 5.**

Carla has 3 vases.
She puts 5 flowers into each vase.
How many flowers are there in all?

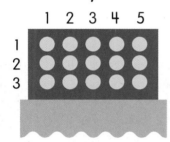

$3 \times 5 = 15$

There are 15 flowers in all.

## Guided Practice

**Use dot paper to find the missing numbers.**

1. Tim has 2 fish tanks.
Each tank has 5 goldfish.
How many goldfish are there in all?

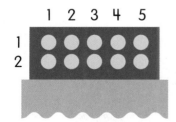

$$\boxed{\phantom{0}} \times \boxed{\phantom{0}} = \boxed{\phantom{0}}$$

There are ⬚ goldfish in all.

# Math Journal

**Look at the picture.**

**1** Use multiplication sentences to tell your friends a story about the birds and nests.

Write a multiplication sentence to find the number of birds.

**Try this.**

**2** Make up your own multiplication story. Ask a classmate to solve it.

---

**Learn**

## You can use short cuts to find multiplication facts.

$3 \times 5 = ?$

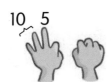

One finger stands for 5.
Two fingers stand for 10.
Three fingers stand for
$10 + 5 = 15$.

$3 \times 5 = 10 + 5$
$\quad\quad = 15$

---

$7 \times 5 = ?$

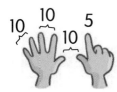

10, 20, 30, 35
$7 \times 5 = 35$

$7 \times 5 = 10 + 10 + 10 + 5$
$\quad\quad = 35$

## Guided Practice

**Use a short cut to find the missing numbers.**

**2**   $4 \times 5 = ?$      $4 \times 5 = $ [ ]

 **WORKING TOGETHER** **Game**

# Spin and Multiply

Players: 4–6
You need:
• cards
• a paper clip
• a pencil

**STEP 1** Each player has a card.

**STEP 2** Place a pencil and a paper clip at the center of the card. Player 1 spins the paper clip.

**STEP 3** The paper clip points towards a number. Player 1 multiplies the number by 5 and writes the answer on the card.

**STEP 4** The other players check the answer.

**STEP 5** Players take turns.

.................................................
: The first player to complete :
: the card wins! :
.................................................

## Multiplication Table of 5

| | | | | |
|---|---|---|---|---|
| 1 | × | 5 | = | 5 |
| 2 | × | 5 | = | 10 |
| 3 | × | 5 | = | 15 |
| 4 | × | 5 | = | 20 |
| 5 | × | 5 | = | 25 |
| 6 | × | 5 | = | 30 |
| 7 | × | 5 | = | 35 |
| 8 | × | 5 | = | 40 |
| 9 | × | 5 | = | 45 |
| 10 | × | 5 | = | 50 |

 **You can multiply numbers in any order.**

$2 \times 5 = 10$

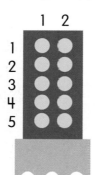

$5 \times 2 = 10$

$2 \times 5 = 5 \times 2$
These are related multiplication facts.

## Guided Practice

**Use dot paper to find the missing numbers.**

3 ⬜ × ⬜ = 20          ⬜ × ⬜ = 20

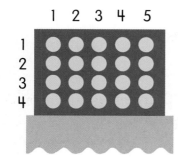          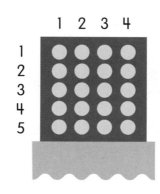

## Let's Explore!

Multiply each number by 5.

|       | 2 | 4 | 6 | 8 | 10 |
|-------|---|---|---|---|----|
| × 5   |   |   |   |   |    |

Do you see any pattern in your answers?

Describe the pattern.

Now, multiply these numbers by 5.

|       | 1 | 3 | 5 | 7 | 9 |
|-------|---|---|---|---|---|
| × 5   |   |   |   |   |   |

Do you see any pattern in your answers?

Describe the pattern.

# Let's Practice

**Use dot paper to find the missing numbers.**

1. $3 \times 5 =$      $5 \times 3 =$

2. $8 \times 5 =$      $5 \times 8 =$

3. $6 \times 5 =$      $5 \times 6 =$

4. $9 \times 5 =$      $5 \times 9 =$

ON YOUR OWN

**Go to Workbook A:
Practice 4, pages 137–140**

# Multiplying 10: Skip-counting and Using Dot Paper

## Lesson Objectives

- Skip-count and use dot paper to multiply by 10.
- Use known multiplication facts to find new multiplication facts.
- Identify related multiplication facts.
- Solve multiplication word problems.

### Learn **You can use a hundreds chart to count by 10.**

Carrie counts the animals at the zoo ten at a time.
Then she colors the number on the hundreds chart.
This is what her chart looks like.

| 1 | 2 | 3 | 4 | 5 | 6 | 7 | 8 | 9 | 10 |
|----|----|----|----|----|----|----|----|----|-----|
| 11 | 12 | 13 | 14 | 15 | 16 | 17 | 18 | 19 | 20 |
| 21 | 22 | 23 | 24 | 25 | 26 | 27 | 28 | 29 | 30 |
| 31 | 32 | 33 | 34 | 35 | 36 | 37 | 38 | 39 | 40 |
| 41 | 42 | 43 | 44 | 45 | 46 | 47 | 48 | 49 | 50 |
| 51 | 52 | 53 | 54 | 55 | 56 | 57 | 58 | 59 | 60 |
| 61 | 62 | 63 | 64 | 65 | 66 | 67 | 68 | 69 | 70 |
| 71 | 72 | 73 | 74 | 75 | 76 | 77 | 78 | 79 | 80 |
| 81 | 82 | 83 | 84 | 85 | 86 | 87 | 88 | 89 | 90 |
| 91 | 92 | 93 | 94 | 95 | 96 | 97 | 98 | 99 | 100 |

What pattern do you see in the colored numbers on the chart?

## Guided Practice

**Continue each skip-counting pattern.**
**Use a hundreds chart to help you.**

1 ⬛ , ⬛ , 80, 70, ⬛ , ⬛ , 40, ⬛ , 20, 10

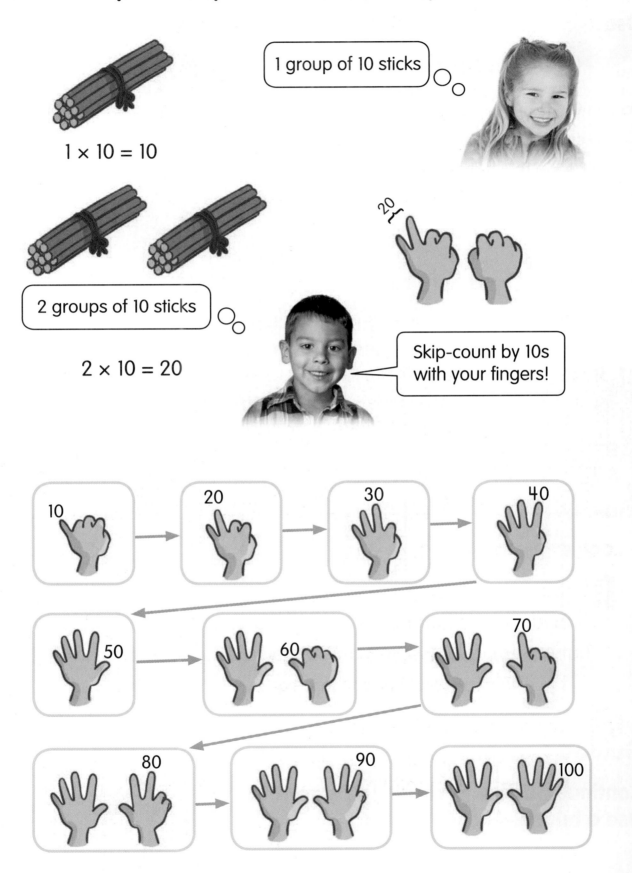

1 group of 10 sticks

$1 \times 10 = 10$

2 groups of 10 sticks

$2 \times 10 = 20$

Skip-count by 10s with your fingers!

10   20   30   40

50   60   70

80   90   100

# Guided Practice

**Use skip-counting to find the missing numbers.**

**2** There are 6 trucks.
Each truck has 10 wheels.
How many wheels are there in all?

6 groups of 10 wheels ○○

I count by 10s.

10, 20, ▢ , ▢ ,

▢ , ▢

▢ × ▢ = ▢

There are ▢ wheels in all.

---

READING AND WRITING MATH
# Math Journal

**Look at each picture.**

**1** Tell a story about the baskets
and the popcorn boxes.

Write a multiplication sentence to
find the number of popcorn boxes.

**2** Tell a story about the tiles and footprints.

Write a multiplication sentence to find
the number of footprints.

## Multiplication Table of 10

| | | | | |
|---|---|---|---|---|
| 1 | × | 10 | = | 10 |
| 2 | × | 10 | = | 20 |
| 3 | × | 10 | = | 30 |
| 4 | × | 10 | = | 40 |
| 5 | × | 10 | = | 50 |
| 6 | × | 10 | = | 60 |
| 7 | × | 10 | = | 70 |
| 8 | × | 10 | = | 80 |
| 9 | × | 10 | = | 90 |
| 10 | × | 10 | = | 100 |

**Learn** You can multiply in any order.

$3 \times 10 = 30$

$10 \times 3 = 30$

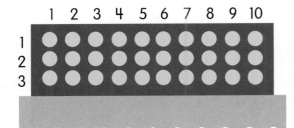

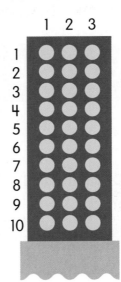

$3 \times 10 = 10 \times 3$
These are related multiplication facts.

## Guided Practice

**Use dot paper to find the missing numbers.**

**3**  [____] × [____] = 80          [____] × [____] = 80

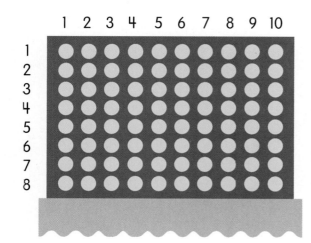 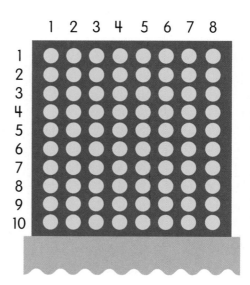

**Use dot paper to find the missing numbers.**

**4**  6 × 10 = [____]          10 × 6 = [____]

**5**  9 × 10 = [____]          10 × 9 = [____]

## Let's Practice

**Multiply.**

**1**  5 × 10 = [____]          **2**  7 × 10 = [____]

**3**  10 × 4 = [____]          **4**  10 × 9 = [____]

# Write multiplication sentences to find the number of dots.

**5**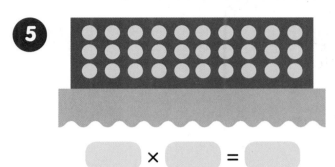

$$\boxed{\phantom{00}} \times \boxed{\phantom{00}} = \boxed{\phantom{00}}$$

**6**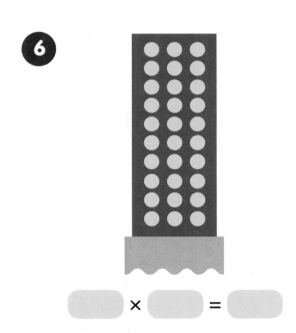

$$\boxed{\phantom{00}} \times \boxed{\phantom{00}} = \boxed{\phantom{00}}$$

## Solve.

**7** 4 groups of children visit a museum.
There are 10 children in each group.
How many children are there altogether?

**8** Marlee and her 7 friends each have 10 tokens for a funfair.
How many tokens do they have altogether?

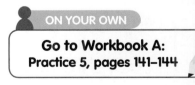

ON YOUR OWN

**Go to Workbook A:
Practice 5, pages 141–144**

# LESSON 6 Divide Using Related Multiplication Facts

## Lesson Objectives

- Use related multiplication facts to find related division facts.
- Write a multiplication sentence and a related division sentence.
- Solve division word problems.

**Learn You can use related multiplication facts to help you divide when you share equally.**

Divide 12 sharpeners into 2 equal groups.
How many sharpeners are in each group?

$12 \div 2 = ?$

$6 \times 2 = 12$
So, $12 \div 2 = 6$.

6 sharpeners are in each group.

## Guided Practice

**Find the missing numbers.**
**Use related multiplication facts to help you divide.**

1. 5 children share 10 cherries equally.
   How many cherries does each child get?

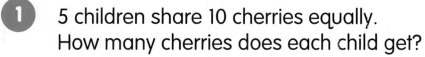

$10 \div 5 = $ 

$\boxed{\phantom{0}} \times 5 = 10$

So, $10 \div 5 = \boxed{\phantom{0}}$.

Each child gets [ ] cherries.

**2**   Kelly puts 40 eggs equally on 10 trays.
How many eggs are on each tray?

40 ÷ 10 = ⬜

⬜ eggs are on each tray.

⬜ × 10 = 40

So, 40 ÷ 10 = ⬜.

**Learn** **You can use related multiplication facts to help you divide when you put things in equal groups.**

Divide 35 cubes into equal groups.
There are 5 cubes in each group.
How many groups are there?

7 × 5 = 35
So, 35 ÷ 5 = 7.

35 ÷ 5 = ?

There are 7 groups.

# Guided Practice

## Use related multiplication facts to find the missing numbers.

**3** Divide 16 marbles into equal groups.
There are 2 marbles in each group.
How many groups are there?

$16 \div 2 = ?$

There are ⬜ groups.

⬜ × 2 = 16

So, $16 \div 2 =$ ⬜.

**4** Ned has 20 crackers.
He puts them equally onto plates.
He puts 10 crackers on each plate.
How many plates of crackers are there?

$20 \div 10 = ?$

There are ⬜ plates of crackers.

⬜ × 10 = 20

So, $20 \div 10 =$ ⬜.

**Learn** **You can write multiplication sentences and related division sentences.**

Darren has 10 counters.

He puts them in groups of 5.

He writes a multiplication sentence and a related division sentence.

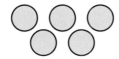 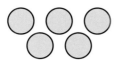

$$2 \times 5 = 10$$
$$10 \div 5 = 2$$

He then puts the counters in groups of 2.

He writes a multiplication sentence and a related division sentence.

$$5 \times 2 = 10$$
$$10 \div 2 = 5$$

$2 \times 5 = 10$   $10 \div 5 = 2$   $5 \times 2 = 10$   $10 \div 2 = 5$

These number sentences are related facts.

## Guided Practice

**Use related multiplication facts to find the missing numbers.**

**5**

$3 \times 2 = $ 〔　　〕        $2 \times 3 = $ 〔　　〕

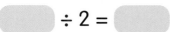 ÷ 2 = 〔　　〕        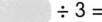 ÷ 3 = 〔　　〕

## Use related multiplication facts to solve.

**6** Sally puts 20 apples equally into 5 boxes.
How many apples are in each box?

**7** Lily has a box of 80 beads.
She uses 10 beads to make one bracelet.
How many bracelets can she make with the box of beads?

**8** Maria puts 14 cubes equally into 2 bags.
How many cubes are in each bag?

**9** Bernard puts 10 marbles equally into 2 groups.
How many marbles are in each group?

## Let's Explore!

Ethan has fewer than 12 chopsticks.
He decides to put them all into groups.
This is what he finds.

First he puts 2 chopsticks in each group.
No chopsticks are left.

Then he puts 5 chopsticks in each group.
No chopsticks are left.

How many chopsticks does Ethan have?

# Let's Practice

**Use related multiplication facts to find the missing numbers.**

**1**  20 ÷ 2 = ⬜

**2**  80 ÷ 10 = ⬜

2 × ⬜ = 20

⬜ × 10 = 80

**Divide.**

**3**  45 ÷ 5 = ⬜

**4**  50 ÷ 10 = ⬜

**Use related multiplication facts to find the missing numbers.**

**5**  4 × 2 = 8    2 × 4 = ⬜    8 ÷ 2 = ⬜    8 ÷ 4 = ⬜

**6**  7 × 5 = 35    5 × 7 = ⬜    35 ÷ 5 = ⬜    35 ÷ 7 = ⬜

**7**  9 × 10 = 90    10 × 9 = ⬜    90 ÷ 10 = ⬜    90 ÷ 9 = ⬜

**Find the missing number.**
**Then, write a related multiplication sentence and two related division sentences for the multiplication sentences.**

**8**  ⬜ × 5 = 20    ⬜ × ⬜ = 20
20 ÷ ⬜ = ⬜    20 ÷ ⬜ = ⬜

**9**  ⬜ × 10 = 60    ⬜ × ⬜ = 60
60 ÷ ⬜ = ⬜    60 ÷ ⬜ = ⬜

## Use related multiplication facts to solve.

**10** Grandma shares 12 apples equally among her grandchildren.
Each grandchild gets 2 apples.
How many grandchildren are there?

**11** Shara has 18 meatballs.
She puts an equal number of meatballs on 2 plates.
How many meatballs are on each plate?

**12** Raja divides 25 chairs equally among 5 tables.
How many chairs are at each table?

**13** Mom makes 50 granola bars.
She packs them into bags of 5.
How many bags of granola bars are there?

**14** The second grade class goes on a bus trip.
There are 40 children in the class.
Each bus can seat 10 children.
How many buses do they need in all?

**15** Sharon picks 90 apples from 10 trees.
She picks the same number of apples from each tree.
How many apples does Sharon pick from each tree?

**ON YOUR OWN**

Go to Workbook A:
Practice 6, pages 145–150

## CRITICAL THINKING SKILLS
# Put On Your Thinking Cap!

**PROBLEM SOLVING**

Alexis has a multiplying machine.
It multiplies the number she puts in by a number.
The new number comes out of the machine.
She puts in six numbers from 1 to 10.
Four numbers come out of the machine.
Two numbers are still inside the machine.

1 Guess the two numbers that will come out.

2 Write the six numbers so they make a pattern.

3 What two possible numbers are still in the machine?

4 By what number does the machine multiply?

5 What number comes out if a 3 is put into the machine?

**ON YOUR OWN**

Go to Workbook A:
Put on Your Thinking Cap!
pages 151–152

# Chapter Wrap Up

BIG IDEA

Known multiplication facts can be used to find other multiplication and division facts.

**You have learned...**

Multiplying 2, 5, and 10 using:

Skip-counting

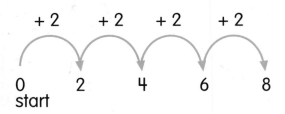

$$4 \times 2 = 8$$

Dot paper

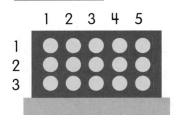

$$3 \times 5 = 15$$

Multiplication tables of 2, 5, and 10.

| | | | | |
|---|---|---|---|---|
| 1 | × | 2 | = | 2 |
| 2 | × | 2 | = | 4 |
| 3 | × | 2 | = | 6 |
| 4 | × | 2 | = | 8 |
| 5 | × | 2 | = | 10 |
| 6 | × | 2 | = | 12 |
| 7 | × | 2 | = | 14 |
| 8 | × | 2 | = | 16 |
| 9 | × | 2 | = | 18 |
| 10 | × | 2 | = | 20 |

| | | | | |
|---|---|---|---|---|
| 1 | × | 5 | = | 5 |
| 2 | × | 5 | = | 10 |
| 3 | × | 5 | = | 15 |
| 4 | × | 5 | = | 20 |
| 5 | × | 5 | = | 25 |
| 6 | × | 5 | = | 30 |
| 7 | × | 5 | = | 35 |
| 8 | × | 5 | = | 40 |
| 9 | × | 5 | = | 45 |
| 10 | × | 5 | = | 50 |

| | | | | |
|---|---|---|---|---|
| 1 | × | 10 | = | 10 |
| 2 | × | 10 | = | 20 |
| 3 | × | 10 | = | 30 |
| 4 | × | 10 | = | 40 |
| 5 | × | 10 | = | 50 |
| 6 | × | 10 | = | 60 |
| 7 | × | 10 | = | 70 |
| 8 | × | 10 | = | 80 |
| 9 | × | 10 | = | 90 |
| 10 | × | 10 | = | 100 |

to multiply numbers in any order.

$$3 \times 2 = 6$$

$$2 \times 3 = 6$$

to use multiplication facts you know to find new multiplication facts.

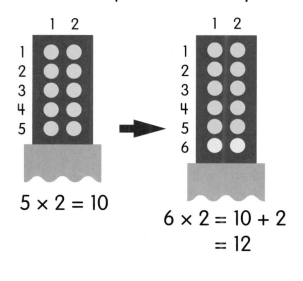

$5 \times 2 = 10$

$6 \times 2 = 10 + 2$
$= 12$

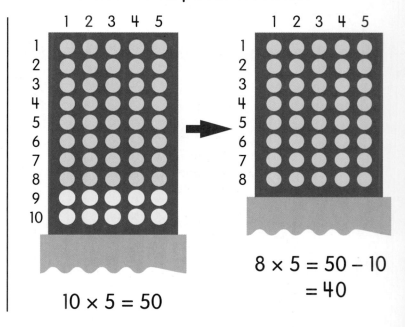

$10 \times 5 = 50$

$8 \times 5 = 50 - 10$
$= 40$

to divide using a related multiplication fact.

$20 \div 4 = 5$

$5 \times 4 = 20$
So, $20 \div 4 = 5$.

to write multiplication sentences and related division sentences.

| | | |
|---|---|---|
| $6 \times 2 = 12$ | $3 \times 5 = 15$ | $8 \times 10 = 80$ |
| $2 \times 6 = 12$ | $5 \times 3 = 15$ | $10 \times 8 = 80$ |
| So, $12 \div 2 = 6$ | So, $15 \div 5 = 3$ | So, $80 \div 10 = 8$ |
| $12 \div 6 = 2$ | $15 \div 3 = 5$ | $80 \div 8 = 10$ |

to solve multiplication and division word problems.

ON YOUR OWN

**Go to Workbook A:
Chapter Review/Test,
pages 153–156**

# CHAPTER 7
# Metric Measurement of Length

**BIG IDEA**

Centimeter rulers and metersticks can be used to measure and compare how long and how tall things are.

# Recall Prior Knowledge

---

### Finding and comparing length in non-standard units

1  stands for 1 unit.

The pencil is about 5 units long.
The length of the pencil is
about 5 units.

The pencil case is about 8 units long.
The length of the pencil case is
about 8 units.

The pencil case is longer than the pencil.
The pencil is shorter than the pencil case.

---

### Adding and subtracting without regrouping

25 + 14 = 39

132 + 53 = 185

```
    1 3 2
 +    5 3
  ───────
    1 8 5
```

78 − 36 = 42

169 − 38 = 131

```
    1 6 9
 −    3 8
  ───────
    1 3 1
```

---

### Adding and subtracting with regrouping

79 + 46 = 125

258 + 347 = 605

```
    ¹ ¹
    2 5 8
 +  3 4 7
  ───────
    6 0 5
```

95 − 47 = 48

231 − 108 = 123

```
      ²
    2 ̶3 ¹1
 −  1 0 8
  ───────
    1 2 3
```

## Quick Check

### Find the missing numbers.

1  stands for 1 unit.

**1**

The diary is about [____] units long.

**2**

The ribbon is about [____] units long.

### Add or subtract.

**3** 71 + 25 = [____]

**4** 53 − 22 = [____]

**5** 613 + 62 = [____]

**6** 498 − 12 = [____]

**7** 47 + 83 = [____]

**8** 74 − 36 = [____]

**9** 375 + 167 = [____]

**10** 605 − 178 = [____]

# 1 Measuring in Meters

**Lesson Objective**

- Use a meterstick to estimate and measure length.

**Learn** **You can use a meterstick to measure length and height.**

Jada, Patrick and Ken have one table each.
They use a **meterstick** to measure the **length** of the table.

A meterstick is a tool used to measure the length of objects.

The length of my table is less than 1 meter.

The length of my table is 1 meter.

The length of my table is more than 1 meter.

Jada

Patrick

Ken

The **meter** is a **unit** of length.
**m** stands for meter . Read 1 m as one meter.
A meter is a little longer than 3 feet.

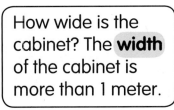
How wide is the cabinet? The **width** of the cabinet is more than 1 meter.

How high is the cabinet? The **height** of the cabinet is about 2 meters.

## Guided Practice

**Look at the drawings.**
**Then fill in the blanks with more or less.**

Metersticks are placed below two bulletin boards.

 Bulletin Board A

Bulletin Board B

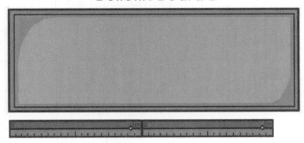

**ⓐ** The length of Bulletin Board A is ⬚ than 1 meter.

**ⓑ** The length of Bulletin Board B is ⬚ than 2 meters.

**Use a meterstick to measure.
Then answer the questions.**

**2** Is the flag pole in front of your school more than or less than 1 meter high?

**3** Name two objects in your school that are about
  **a** 1 meter long          **b** 1 meter high

**4** Name two objects in your home that are
  **a** less than 1 meter          **b** more than 1 meter

 **Hands-On Activity**

WORKING TOGETHER

Use a meterstick or string that is 1 meter long.
First, guess the length of each object.
Then, use the meterstick or string to measure.
What are the two whole numbers of meters that the measurement is between?
Record your answers in a chart.

|  | My guess | The length is between |
|---|---|---|
| The height of your classroom door | about 2 meters | 2 meters and 3 meters |
| The width of your classroom door |  |  |
| The width of a classroom window |  |  |
| The length of your friend's arm span |  |  |
| The length of your teacher's desk |  |  |
| The width of your teacher's desk |  |  |
| The length of the gym floor |  |  |
| The width of the gym floor |  |  |

# Let's Practice

**Use a meterstick to measure.**
**Then answer the questions.**

**1** Is your classroom window more than or less than 1 meter high?

**2** Name two objects that are

**a** less than 1 meter long.

**b** more than 1 meter long.

**3** Write the names of five objects on a chart.
Measure the lengths of the objects.
Then put a check in the correct box.

| Object | Less than 1 meter | 1 meter | More than 1 meter |
|--------|-------------------|---------|-------------------|
| Shoe   | ✓                 |         |                   |
|        |                   |         |                   |
|        |                   |         |                   |
|        |                   |         |                   |
|        |                   |         |                   |
|        |                   |         |                   |

**ON YOUR OWN**

**Go to Workbook A:**
**Practice 1, pages 165–168**

# LESSON

# 2 Comparing Lengths in Meters

## Lesson Objectives

- Compare lengths.
- Find the difference in lengths of objects.

**Vocabulary**

taller    shorter    longer

tallest    shortest    longest

**Learn** **You can use meters to compare heights.**

Mrs. Cole, Mrs. Ruiz, and Mrs. Lee have fences around their yards. How can you find out whose fence is the **tallest** ?

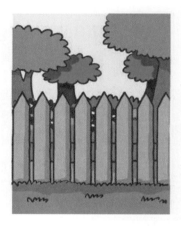

Mrs. Cole's fence     Mrs. Ruiz's fence     Mrs. Lee's fence

I cannot tell which fence is **taller** because I cannot put them side by side.

You can compare by measuring their heights in meters. Then, subtract to find the difference in their heights.

# You can use meters to compare lengths.

This fence is 2 meters tall.

This fence is 1 meter tall.
2 − 1 = 1
So, Mrs. Cole's fence is 1 meter taller than Mrs. Ruiz's fence.

This fence is more than 2 meters tall. Mrs. Lee's fence is the tallest and Mrs. Ruiz's fence is the **shortest**.

This car is about 3 meters long.

This van is about 5 meters long.
5 − 3 = 2
The car is 2 meters **shorter** than the van.
The van is 2 meters **longer** than the car.

This truck is the **longest**. It is about 11 meters long!

1 m

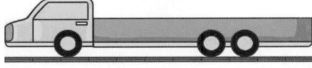

## Guided Practice

**Answer each question.**

**1** A blue ribbon is 8 meters long.

A red ribbon is 3 meters long.

**a** Which ribbon is longer?

**b** How much longer?

## 👋 Hands-On Activity

**1** Use a meterstick to help you answer each question.
Is the chalkboard in your classroom longer or shorter than the meterstick?
Is your schoolbag longer or shorter than the meterstick?
Which is longer, the chalkboard or your schoolbag?

**2** Choose two objects that can be found in your classroom.
Use a meterstick to find out which of the two objects is shorter.

## Guided Practice

**Answer each question.**

**2** Barry has two ropes.
Rope A is 12 meters long.
Rope B is 8 meters long.

   **a** Which rope is longer?

   **b** How much longer is it?

# Let's Practice

**Solve.**

**1** An apple tree is 11 meters tall.
A peach tree is 5 meters tall.

   **a** Which tree is shorter?

   **b** How much shorter is it?

**2** The length of an ice skating rink is 25 meters.
The length of a swimming pool is 50 meters.

   **a** Which is longer?

   **b** How much longer is it?

**Solve.**

**3**

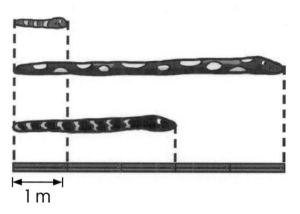

1 m

**ⓐ** Which is the longest snake?

**ⓑ** What is the difference in length between the shortest and the longest snakes?

**4**

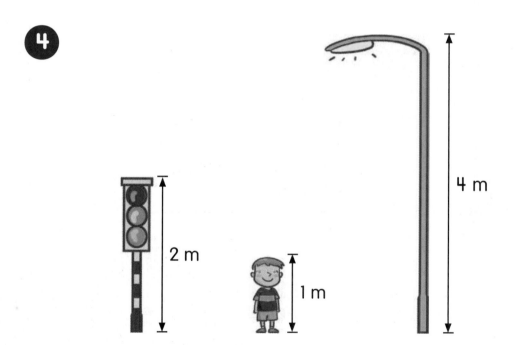

4 m

2 m

1 m

**ⓐ** Which is the tallest?

**ⓑ** How much taller is the street light than the traffic light?

**ⓒ** How much shorter is the boy than the street light?

ON YOUR OWN

Go to Workbook A:
Practice 2, pages 169–170

# LESSON

# 3 Measuring in Centimeters

**Lesson Objectives**

- Use a centimeter ruler to measure length.
- Draw a line of given length.

**Vocabulary**
centimeter (cm)

**Learn**

## You can use centimeters to measure lengths of shorter objects.

This is a centimeter ruler.

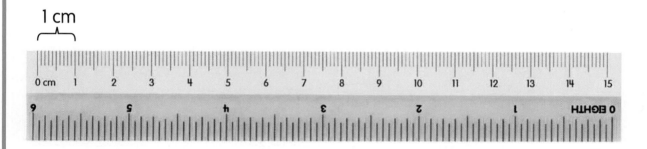

1 cm

What is centimeter?

It is a unit of length like the meter.
You can use it to measure shorter objects.

A **centimeter** is a unit of length.
**cm** stands for centimeter.
Read 1 cm as one centimeter.
A centimeter is used to measure shorter length.

Continued on next page

The lengths between the centimeter markings are equal.

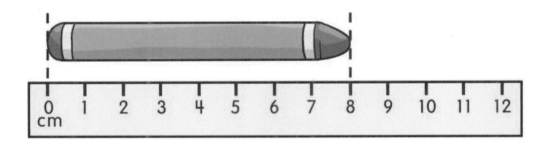

To measure the length of an object, put the object above the zero mark on the ruler.

Then, read the marking on the ruler where the object ends. The length of the crayon is 8 centimeters.

# Guided Practice

## Look at the pictures.

**1** Which shows the correct way of measuring objects? A, B, or C?

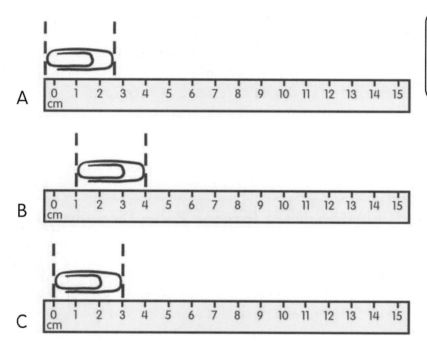

These rulers are smaller than in real life.

## Find the missing numbers.

**2**

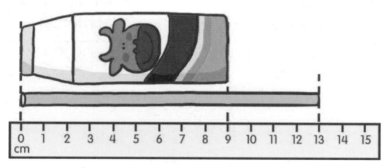

**a** The length of the carton of milk is ⬜ centimeters.

**b** The length of the straw is ⬜ centimeters.

**Guess the lengths of the objects in centimeters.**
**Then measure the objects.**
**Write your answers in a chart.**

**3**

| Object | My guess | The length is between |
|---|---|---|
| pencil | about ___ cm | ___ cm and ___ cm |
| eraser | about ___ cm | ___ cm and ___ cm |

**Draw a line 4 centimeters long.**
**Name it Drawing A.**
**Then draw Drawing B, 5 centimeters longer than Drawing A.**

**4** Find the length of Drawing B. ___ cm

**Find the missing number.**

**5** Look at the curve below.
Place a string along the curve.
Cut a piece of string as long as the curve.
Then place the string on a ruler to find its length in centimeters.

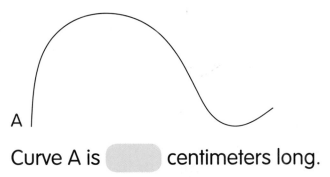

A

Curve A is ___ centimeters long.

# Hands-On Activity

**STEP 1**

Use two strips of paper of different lengths.

**STEP 2**

Measure the length of each strip with a ruler.
Write the length of each strip on the strip.

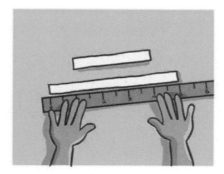

**STEP 3**

Find out who else in the class has strips that are
the same length as yours.

**Jerome and Tracie are measuring the lengths of their books.**

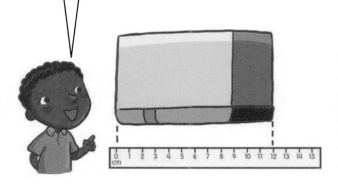

The length of my book is 12 centimeters.

The length of my book is less than 12 centimeters

Who is correct?
Explain your answer.

These rulers are smaller than in real life.

**You can use a centimeter tape to measure height and length around objects.**

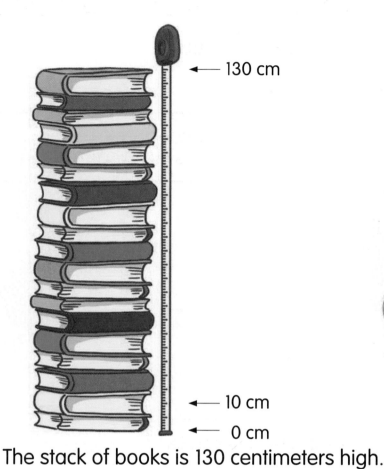

← 130 cm

← 10 cm

← 0 cm

The stack of books is 130 centimeters high.

The length around my head is 35 centimeters.

## Guided Practice

**Find the missing numbers.**

**a** The pencil case is ⬜ centimeters long.

**b** The pencil case is ⬜ centimeters wide.

# Learn You can measure objects using a different start point.

Oh no! My ruler is broken. How do I use it to find the length of the sharpener?

You can subtract to find the length of the sharpener.
$8 - 4 = 4$
The sharpener is 4 centimeters long.

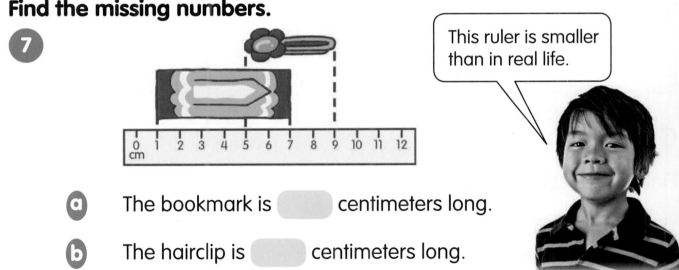

## Guided Practice

**Find the missing numbers.**

**7**

This ruler is smaller than in real life.

**a**    The bookmark is ⬭ centimeters long.

**b**    The hairclip is ⬭ centimeters long.

# Let's Practice

## Answer the question.

What is the length of each ribbon?
Use a centimeter ruler to find out.

**1** Ribbon A

[____] cm

**2** Ribbon B

[____] cm

## Cut a piece of string as long as the drawing.
## Then place the string on a centimeter ruler to find its length.

**3** The length of the drawing is [____] centimeters.

**4** The length of the drawing is [____] centimeters.

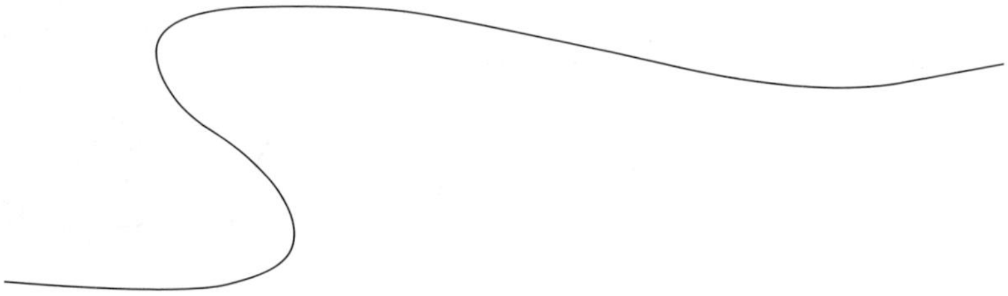

**5** The length of the drawing is ▢ centimeters.

**6** Follow these steps, then answer the question.

**a** Draw a line 10 centimeters long.
Name it Drawing A.

**b** Draw a line 3 centimeters longer than Drawing A.
Name it Drawing B.

**c** Draw a line 5 centimeters shorter than Drawing B.
Name it Drawing C.

**d** What is the length of Drawing C? ▢ centimeters

## Find the missing numbers.

**7**

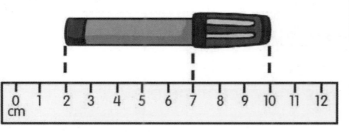

This ruler is smaller than in real life.

**a** The marker is ▢ centimeters long.

**b** The cap of the marker is ▢ centimeters long.

ON YOUR OWN

**Go to Workbook A:**
**Practice 3, pages 171–174**

# LESSON 4 Comparing Lengths in Centimeters

## Lesson Objectives

- Use a centimeter ruler to measure and compare lengths of objects.
- Find the difference in centimeters in lengths of objects.

**Learn** **You can measure objects in centimeters to compare their lengths.**

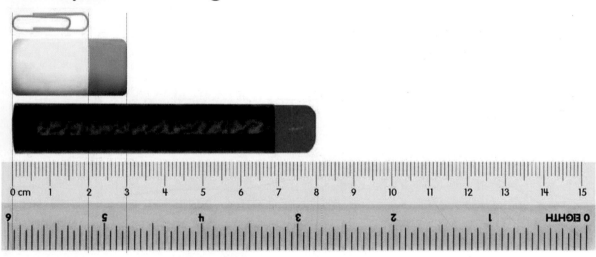

The paper clip is 2 centimeters long.
The eraser is 3 centimeters long.
The crayon is 8 centimeters long.

The eraser is longer than the paper clip.
$3 - 2 = 1$
It is 1 centimeter longer.

The crayon is longer than the eraser.
$8 - 3 = 5$
It is 5 centimeters longer.

The eraser is shorter than the crayon.
$8 - 3 = 5$
It is 5 centimeters shorter.

The paper clip is shortest and the crayon is longest.

> You can subtract to find the difference in lengths.

# Guided Practice

**Find the missing numbers.**

**1**

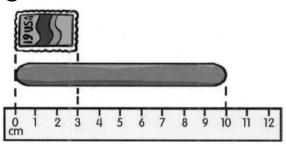

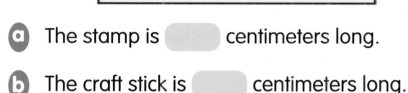

These rulers are smaller than in real life.

**ⓐ** The stamp is [     ] centimeters long.

**ⓑ** The craft stick is [     ] centimeters long.

**ⓒ** [     ] – [     ] = [     ]

The stamp is [     ] centimeters shorter than the craft stick.

**2**

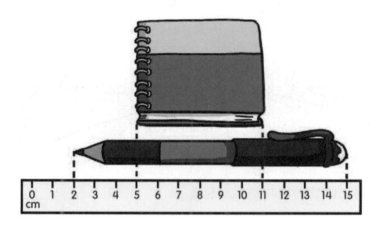

**ⓐ** Length of pen: 15 – 2 = 13

The pen is [     ] centimeters long.

**ⓑ** Length of notebook: 11 – [     ] = [     ]

The notebook is [     ] centimeters long.

**ⓒ** Difference in length: [     ] – [     ] = [     ]

The pen is [     ] centimeters longer than the notebook.

## Guided Practice

**Find the missing words and numbers.**

**3**   Use a ruler to measure the lengths of these ribbons.

Ribbon A

Ribbon B

**a**   Ribbon A is [ ] centimeters long.

**b**   Ribbon B is [ ] centimeters long.

**c**   Ribbon [ ] is longer than Ribbon [ ].

**d**   How much longer? [ ] centimeters

## ✋ Hands-On Activity

**STEP 1**   Find the length of your math book.

**STEP 2**   Then, find the length of your pencil.
Which is shorter, the pencil or the math book?
How much shorter is it?

**STEP 3**   Measure the lengths of two other objects.
What is the length of the longer object?
How much longer is it?

# Let's Practice

**Use a string and a ruler to measure.
Then answer the question.**

**1** Which is longer, the toothbrush or the ribbon?

The ⬜ is longer.

**Use the picture to answer each question.**

**2**

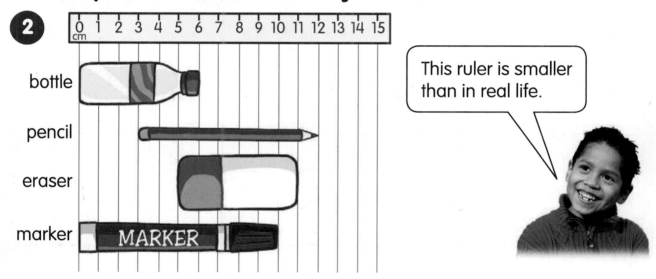

This ruler is smaller than in real life.

**a** What is the length of the marker? ⬜ cm

**b** Which is longer, the pencil or the marker? ⬜

**c** The longest item is the ⬜.

**d** Which two items have the same length? ⬜

**Andrew wrote the following in his book.**
**Help him fill in the blanks with cm or m.**

**3** Height of flag pole = 7 [  ]

**4** Length of field = 50 [  ]

**5** Length of insect = 5 [  ]

**6** Length of spoon = 14 [  ]

**Use a ruler to measure the length of the crayon and the spoon.**

**7**

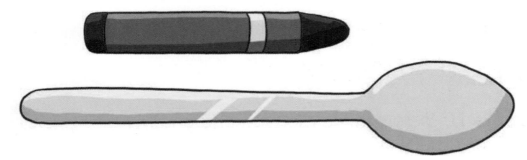

**a** How long is the crayon? [  ]

**b** How long is the spoon? [  ]

**c** Which is longer? [  ]

**d** How much longer? [  ]

**8** Find the lengths of the drawings in each set.

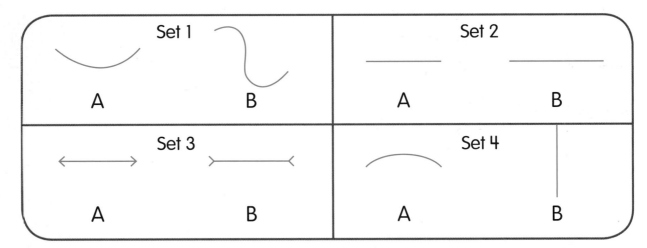

| Set 1 | Set 2 |
|---|---|
| A          B | A          B |
| Set 3 | Set 4 |
| A          B | A          B |

**a** Which set has two drawings with the same length? [  ]

**b** For each of the other three sets, which drawing is longer?

In set [  ] , drawing [  ] is longer.

In set [  ] , drawing [  ] is longer.

In set [  ] , drawing [  ] is longer.

ON YOUR OWN

Go to Workbook A:
Practice 4, pages 175–178

**LESSON**
**5**

# Real-World Problems: Metric Length

## Lesson Objectives

- Solve one-step and two-step problems involving length.
- Draw models to solve real-world problems.

**Learn** **You can use bar models to solve measurement problems in meters.**

Jane walks 20 meters in the morning and another 35 meters in the evening.

**a** How far does Jane walk in all?

**b** How much more does she walk in the evening?

**a**
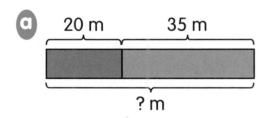

20 + 35 = 55
Jane walks 55 meters in all.

**b**

35 − 20 = 15
She walks 15 meters more in the evening.

Morning 20 m

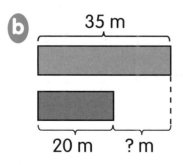

Evening 35 m

# Guided Practice

**Solve.**

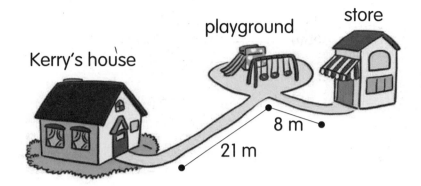

Kerry's house    playground    store

8 m

21 m

Kerry walks from her house to the store.
On her way, she passes the playground.
How far does she walk in all?

 +  =

She walks ⬜ meters in all.

m    m

? m

2   lighthouse

12 m

40 m

How far is the swimmer from the lighthouse?

 −  =

The swimmer is ⬜ meters from
the lighthouse.

40 m

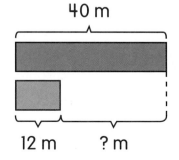

12 m    ? m

**You can use bar models to solve measurement problems in centimeters.**

Nikki has a cloth that is 45 centimeters long.
She cuts it into three pieces.
The first piece is 15 centimeters long.
The second piece is 12 centimeters long.

**ⓐ** Find the total length of the first and second pieces.

**ⓑ** What is the length of the third piece?

**ⓐ**

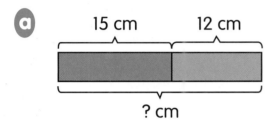

$$15 + 12 = 27$$

The total length of the first and second pieces is 27 centimeters.

**ⓑ**

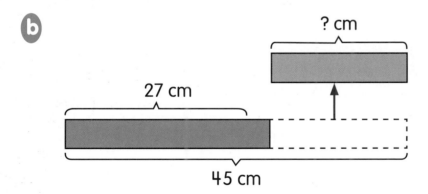

$$45 - 27 = 18$$

The length of the third piece is 18 centimeters.

# Guided Practice

**Solve.**

**3** Liza has a red ribbon 100 centimeters long.
She cuts 36 centimeters off the ribbon.
Then she joins a blue ribbon, 75 centimeters long,
to the remaining red ribbon.
What is the total length of the ribbons now?

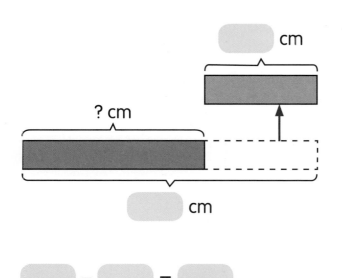

How long was the piece of red ribbon that was left?

( ) − ( ) = ( )

The length of the red ribbon she has left is ( ) centimeters.

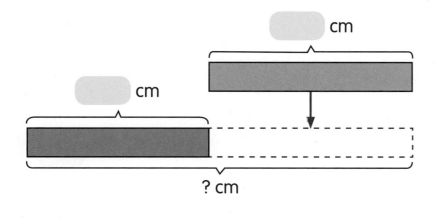

Now find the length of the red and blue ribbon.

( ) + ( ) = ( )

The total length of the the ribbons is now ( ) centimeters.

# Let's Practice

**Solve.**

**1** Tony jogs two times around a 400-meter track.
How far does he jog in meters?

**2** The length of Adam's notebook is 21 centimeters.
Hector's notebook is 5 centimeters longer.
How long is Hector's notebook?

**3** A string that is 20 centimeters long is cut into two pieces.
One piece is 8 centimeters long.
How long is the other piece?

**4** Harry's string is 25 centimeters long.
Keisha's string is 12 centimeters longer.
How long is Keisha's string?

**5** A tall room has two windows, one above the other.
The bottom window is 162 centimeters tall.
The top window is 47 centimeters shorter.

**a** How tall is the top window?

**b** What is the height of both windows?

**6** A rope 42 meters long is cut into two pieces.
The first piece is 14 meters.

**a** How long is the second piece?

**b** What is the difference in length
between the two pieces?

**ON YOUR OWN**

**Go to Workbook A:
Practice 5, pages 179–182**

**PROBLEM SOLVING**

Nina enters the supermarket.
She wants to get to the meat section.
She can only walk down any path once.

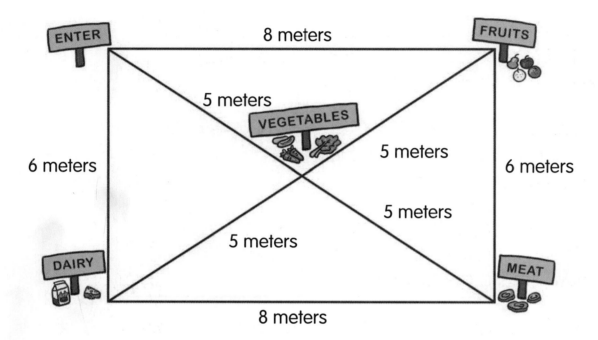

1   She has walked 14 meters when she reaches the meat section.
    One path she can take is Enter ⟶ Dairy ⟶ Meat.
    Name the other path she can take.

2   From Enter, if she walks 22 meters, which path does she take?

3   From Enter, if she walks 26 meters, which path does she take?

4   Describe another path Nina can take from Enter.

5   Is there another path that has the
    same length? Explain your answer.

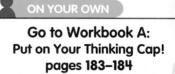
ON YOUR OWN

Go to Workbook A:
Put on Your Thinking Cap!
pages 183–184

# Chapter Wrap Up

**You have learned...**

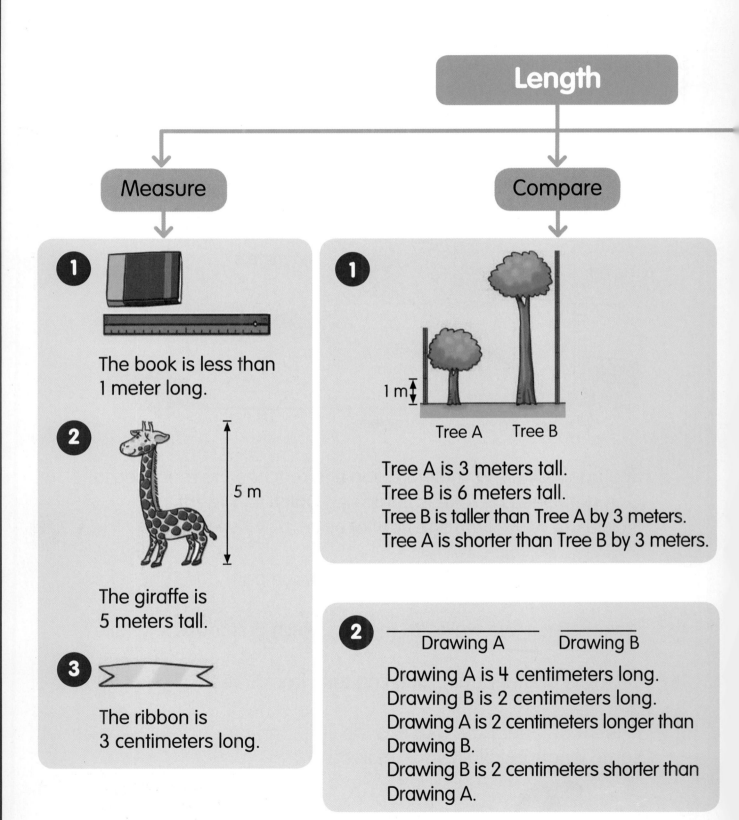

Length

Measure

**1** The book is less than 1 meter long.

**2** 5 m

The giraffe is 5 meters tall.

**3** The ribbon is 3 centimeters long.

Compare

**1**

1 m

Tree A    Tree B

Tree A is 3 meters tall.
Tree B is 6 meters tall.
Tree B is taller than Tree A by 3 meters.
Tree A is shorter than Tree B by 3 meters.

**2** Drawing A    Drawing B

Drawing A is 4 centimeters long.
Drawing B is 2 centimeters long.
Drawing A is 2 centimeters longer than Drawing B.
Drawing B is 2 centimeters shorter than Drawing A.

BIG IDEA

Centimeter rulers and metersticks can be used to measure and compare how long and how tall things are.

Solve real-world problems

**1** Mr. Lee has 17 meters of cloth in his shop.
He sells 9 meters of cloth.
How many meters of
cloth does he have now?

$17 - 9 = 8$
He has 8 meters of cloth left.

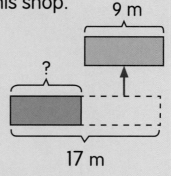

**2** Rosita has 15 centimeters of tape.
She needs 3 centimeters more tape to wrap a gift.
How much tape does she need to wrap the gift?

$3 + 15 = 18$
She needs 18 centimeters of tape.

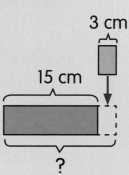

ON YOUR OWN

**Go to Workbook A:**
Chapter Review/Test,
pages 185–190

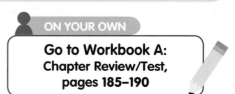

# CHAPTER 8 Mass

Look! Aunt Carol sent us a cookbook from England!

All the ingredients in the recipes are measured in grams and kilograms!

I think we can use this scale to measure the ingredients.

I see why. This scale can measure in pounds and ounces or kilograms and grams.

We have 2 kilograms of flour but we only need 1 kilogram.

FLOUR

Recipe

BUTTER

The muffins are ready!

**BIG IDEA**

A scale can be used to measure and compare masses in kilograms and grams.

# Recall Prior Knowledge

## Comparing weights of objects on a balance

The chick is lighter than the hen.
The hen is heavier than the chick.
The cat is heavier than the hen.
The chick is the lightest.
The cat is the heaviest.

## Finding weights of objects in non-standard units

1 ■ stands for 1 unit.

The weight of the orange is about 7 units.

## Adding and subtracting without regrouping

$259 + 130 = 389$

$$
\begin{array}{r}
2\,5\,9 \\
+\,1\,3\,0 \\
\hline
3\,8\,9
\end{array}
$$

$485 - 263 = 222$

$$
\begin{array}{r}
4\,8\,5 \\
-\,2\,6\,3 \\
\hline
2\,2\,2
\end{array}
$$

789 + 123 = 912                    548 − 367 = 181

$$\begin{array}{r} \overset{1}{7}\ \overset{1}{8}\ 9 \\ +\ 1\ 2\ 3 \\ \hline 9\ 1\ 2 \end{array}$$

$$\begin{array}{r} \overset{4}{5}\ \overset{1}{4}\ 8 \\ -\ 3\ 6\ 7 \\ \hline 1\ 8\ 1 \end{array}$$

## ✔ Quick Check

**Answer these questions.**

 1

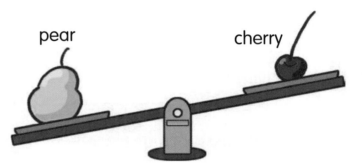

pear          cherry

Which is lighter? ⬭

2

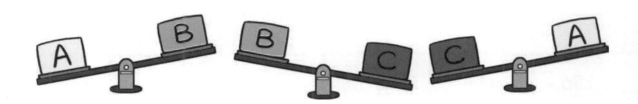

Which box is heaviest? ⬭

# Find the weight of each object.
## 1  represents 1 unit.

**3**

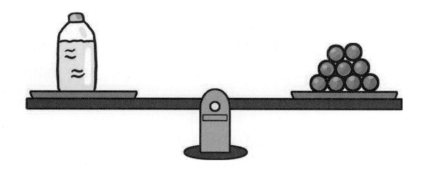

The weight of the bottle of water is about ⬚ units.

**4**

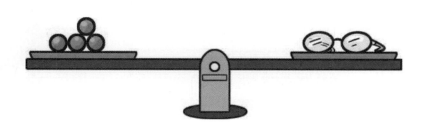

The weight of the glasses is about ⬚ units.

## Add or subtract.

**5**    384 + 225 = ⬚

**6**    576 − 341 = ⬚

**7**    239 + 183 = ⬚

**8**    617 − 424 = ⬚

# 1 Measuring in Kilograms

## Lesson Objective

- Use a measuring scale to measure mass in kilograms.

**Vocabulary**

kilogram (kg)  measuring scale  less than

mass        as heavy as    more than

 **Learn** **You can use a kilogram as a unit of measurement to compare the mass of different objects.**

Use a 1-kilogram mass.

### Step 1
Hold the 1-kilogram mass in your hand.

### Step 2
Next, hold a notebook in your other hand.
Which is heavier, the 1-kilogram mass or the notebook?

### Step 3
Put the notebook down.
Carry your school bag.
Which is heavier, the 1-kilogram mass or the school bag?

The kilogram is a unit of mass.
**kg** stands for kilogram.
Read 1 kg as one kilogram.
A kilogram is used to measure the mass of heavier objects.

# Learn The mass of an object can be equal to 1 kilogram.

What is the mass of the bag of flour?

Read the **measuring scale**. The mass of the bag of flour is 1 kilogram.

The bag of flour is **as heavy as** a mass of 1 kilogram.

# Learn The mass of an object can be less than 1 kilogram.

What can you say about the mass of the box of tissues?

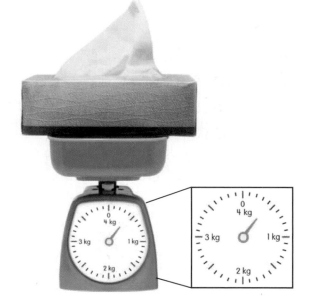

The mass of the box of tissues is **less than** 1 kilogram.

**Learn** The mass of an object can be more than 1 kilogram.

What can you say about the mass of the watermelon?

The mass of the watermelon is **more than** 1 kilogram.

 **Hands-On Activity**

Use a few objects and a scale.

**STEP 1** Guess the mass of each object.
Is it 1 kilogram, less than 1 kilogram, or more than 1 kilogram?
Record your guesses in a chart.

| Name of Object | My Guess | | | Actual Mass | | |
|---|---|---|---|---|---|---|
| | Less than 1 kg | 1 kg | More than 1 kg | Less than 1 kg | 1 kg | More than 1 kg |
| A bag of sugar | | | | | | |
| | | | | | | |

**STEP 2** Use the scale to find the actual mass of each object.
Complete the chart.

**You can use a balance scale to find the mass of objects.**

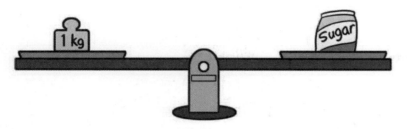

The mass of the bag of sugar is 1 kilogram.

## Guided Practice

**Find the mass of each object in kilograms.**

**1**

The mass of the bag of potatoes is ⬜ kilograms.

**2** The mass of the bag of rice is ⬜ kilogram.

**3** The mass of the bottle of oil is ⬜ kilograms.

# Find the mass of each object in kilograms.

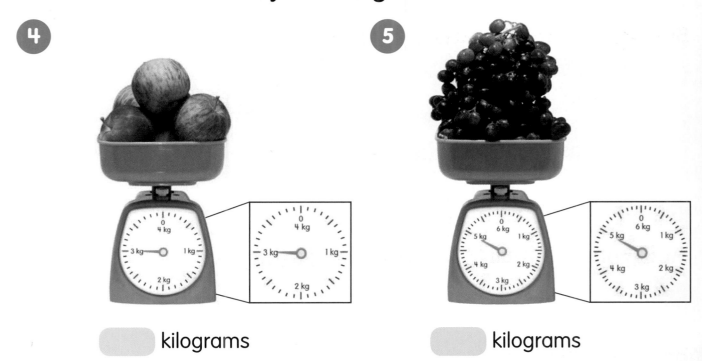

**4**

\_\_\_ kilograms

**5**

\_\_\_ kilograms

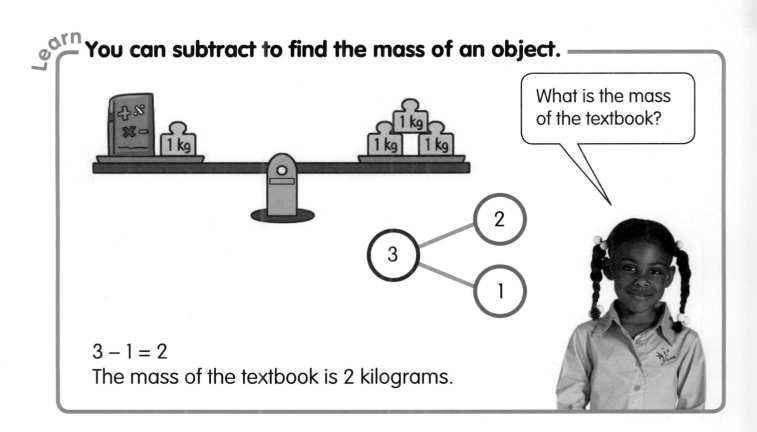

## Learn You can subtract to find the mass of an object.

What is the mass of the textbook?

3 – 1 = 2
The mass of the textbook is 2 kilograms.

## Guided Practice

**Subtract to find the mass in kilograms.**

**6**

( ) − ( ) = ( )

The mass of the watermelon is ( ) kilograms.

# Let's Practice

**Answer these questions.**

tomato

watermelon

pineapple

**1** Which fruit has a mass of 1 kilogram? ( )

**2** Which fruit is less than 1 kilogram? ( )

**3** Which fruit is more than 1 kilogram? ( )

# Find the mass of the fruits in kilograms.

**4**

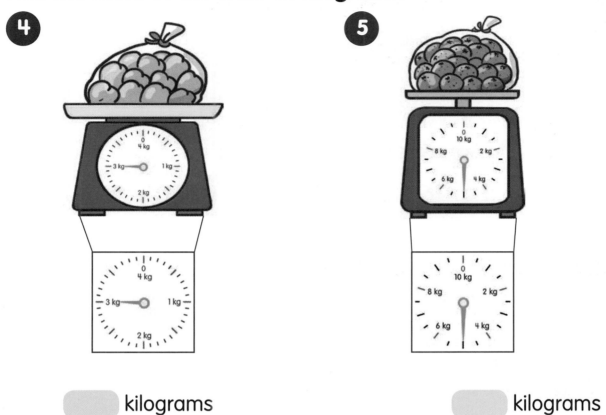

　　　 kilograms

**5**

　　　 kilograms

# Find the mass of the object in kilograms.
# Write a subtraction sentence to help you.

**6**

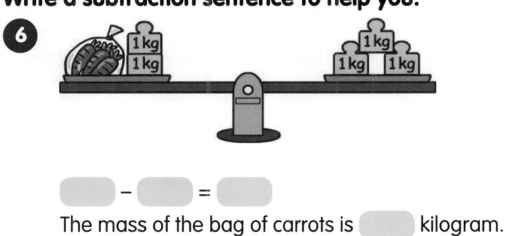

　　　 – 　　　 = 　　　

The mass of the bag of carrots is 　　　 kilogram.

**ON YOUR OWN**

**Go to Workbook A:**
Practice 1, pages 191–192

# Comparing Masses in Kilograms

## Lesson Objective

- Compare and order masses.

> **Vocabulary**
>
> heavier than     heaviest
> lighter than     lightest

### *Learn* You can compare masses in kilograms.

Bag A

Bag B

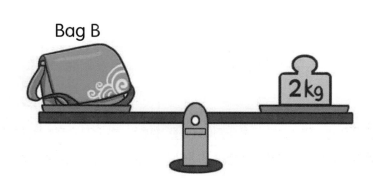

Bag A has a mass of 3 kilograms. Bag B has a mass of 2 kilograms.
Bag A is **heavier than** Bag B.
Bag B is **lighter than** Bag A.

$3 - 2 = 1$
Bag A is 1 kilogram heavier than Bag B.
Bag B is 1 kilogram lighter than Bag A.

$3 + 2 = 5$
The total mass of Bag A and Bag B is 5 kilograms.

# Guided Practice

**Read the measuring scale to find the mass of each object.
Then answer the questions.**

Package X

Package Y

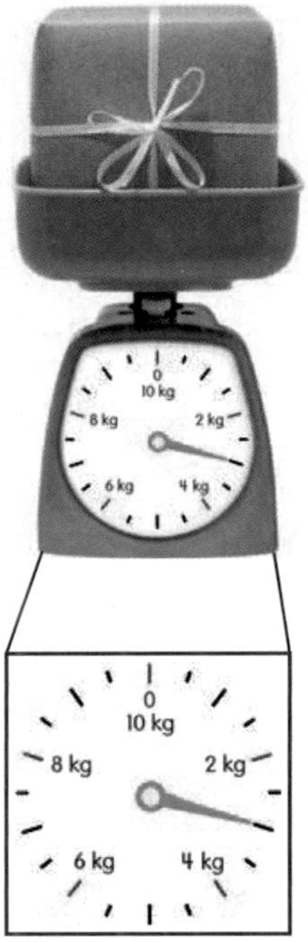

1. The mass of Package X is [        ] kilograms.

2. The mass of Package Y is [     ] kilograms.

3. Which package is heavier? Package [     ]

4. How much heavier? [     ] kilograms

5. The total mass of Package X and Package Y is [     ] kilograms.

# Look at the pictures.
# Then answer the questions.

carrots

apples

cabbage

**6** Which is the **heaviest**?

**7** Which is the **lightest**?

**8** Order the items from lightest to heaviest.

_____ , _____ , _____

lightest

**9**

If the items are put on a balance, is the picture above correct?

Why or why not?

# Let's Practice

**Read the measuring scale to find the mass of each object.
Then answer the questions.**

Bag A    Bag B

**1** The mass of Bag A is ⬚ kilograms.

**2** The mass of Bag B is ⬚ kilograms.

**3** Which bag is heavier? Bag ⬚

**4** How much heavier? ⬚ kilograms heavier

**Look at the pictures.
Then answer the questions.**

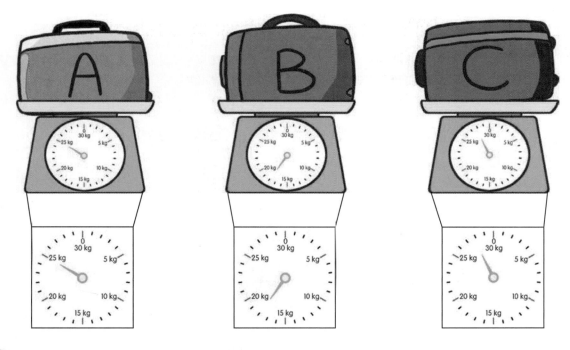

**5** The mass of Bag A is ⬚ kilograms.

**6** The mass of Bag B is ⬚ kilograms.

**7** The mass of Bag C is ⬚ kilograms.

**8** Bag A is ⬚ kilograms heavier than Bag B.

**9** Bag B is ⬚ kilograms lighter than Bag C.

**10** The total mass of Bag A and Bag C is ⬚ kilograms.

**11** Order the bags from heaviest to lightest.

⬚ , ⬚ , ⬚

heaviest

ON YOUR OWN

**Go to Workbook A:
Practice 2, pages 193–196**

# 3 Measuring in Grams

**Lesson Objective**

- Use a measuring scale to measure mass in grams.

**Learn You can use smaller units to measure the mass of lighter objects.**

These are some objects that are lighter than 1 kilogram.

The paper clip has a mass of 1 **gram**.

The pencil has a mass of 5 grams.

> The gram is a unit of mass.
> **g** stands for gram.
> Read 1 g as 1 gram.
> A gram is used to measure the mass of lighter objects.

**Learn** You can use the gram scale to measure the mass of objects less than 1 kilogram.

I use this measuring scale to measure mass less than 500 grams. One small marking stands for 10 grams.

The pencil case has a mass of 300 grams.

The muffin has a mass of 20 grams.

## Guided Practice

**Read the measuring scale to find the mass of each object.**

**1**

The package has a mass of ___ grams.

**2**

The light bulb has a mass of ___ grams.

# Hands-On Activity

**WORKING TOGETHER**

**1** Use a measuring scale to find the masses of six small objects.
Put the objects into three groups.

**a** Masses more than 50 g and less than 100 g.

**b** Masses more than 100 g and less than 500 g.

**c** Masses more than 500 g and less than 900 g.

**2** Work in groups of three or four.
Use beans and a measuring scale.

**a** Use the scale to weigh these amounts of beans.

50 g     100 g     150 g     200 g

250 g     550 g     750 g

**b** Put each amount in a plastic bag.
Write the mass of the beans on each bag.

**c** Which bags make up 1,000 grams?

# Guided Practice

## Choose gram or kilogram.

**3** Which unit would you use to find the mass of the

**a** watermelon?                       **b** eraser?

Eraser

# Let's Practice

**Find the mass of each object in grams.**

**1**

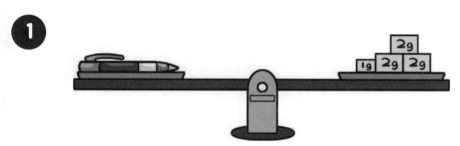

The mass of the pen is ⬤ grams.

**2**

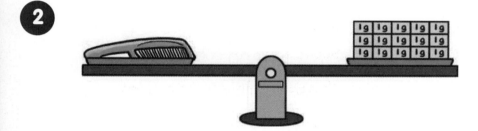

The mass of the comb is ⬤ grams.

**3**

The vegetables have a mass
of ⬤ grams.

**4**

The grapes have a mass
of ⬤ grams.

## Choose kg or g.

**5**

179 ◻

**6**

250 ◻

**7**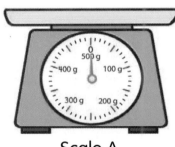

5 ◻

**8**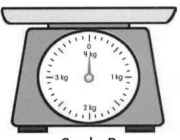

300 ◻

## Which scale would you use to find the mass of each object?

Scale A

Scale B

**9** A nickel: Scale ◻

**10** A basket of fruit: Scale ◻

**11** A laptop computer: Scale ◻

**12** A watch: Scale ◻

ON YOUR OWN

Go to Workbook A:
Practice 3, pages 197–202

# 4 Comparing Masses in Grams

**Lesson Objective**

- Compare and order masses in grams.

**Learn** **You can compare masses in grams.**

The mass of the bag of flour is 250 grams.
The mass of the bag of sugar is 150 grams.
The mass of the bag of rice is 500 grams.

The bag of sugar is the lightest object.
The bag of rice is the heaviest object.
From lightest to heaviest, the objects are: sugar, flour, rice.

You can find the total mass of the bag of flour and the bag of sugar.
250 + 150 = 400
The total mass of the bag of flour and the bag of sugar is 400 grams.

## Guided Practice

Ben is finding the masses of his tape dispenser, stapler, and notebook using a measuring scale.

This is what Ben writes on a piece of paper.

The mass of my tape dispenser is 320 grams.
The mass of my stapler is 100 grams.
The mass of my notebook is 250 grams.
The lightest object is my stapler.
The heaviest object is my tape dispenser.

**Help Ben complete each sentence.**
**Use lighter or heavier.**

1　The notebook is ⬚ than the stapler.

2　The stapler is ⬚ than the tape dispenser.

3　Order the stapler, tape dispenser, and notebook from heaviest to lightest.

　　⬚ , ⬚ , ⬚
　　heaviest

4　The tape dispenser is ⬚ than the total mass of the stapler and the notebook.

> 100 + 250 = 350
> The total mass of the stapler and notebook is 350 grams.

 # Hands-On Activity

Use three bags of marbles labeled X, Y and Z.

**STEP 1** Hold each bag and guess how heavy it is.
Record your guesses in a chart.

**STEP 2** Use a scale to find the actual mass of each bag.
Record on a copy of this chart.

|  | **My Guess** | **Actual Mass** |
|---|---|---|
| Bag X |  |  |
| Bag Y |  |  |
| Bag Z |  |  |

**STEP 3** Complete these sentences.

The heaviest bag has a mass of [    ] grams.

The lightest bag has a mass of [    ] grams.

Put the bags in order from lightest to heaviest.

[    ] , [    ] , [    ]

lightest

**You can subtract to find the difference in mass.**

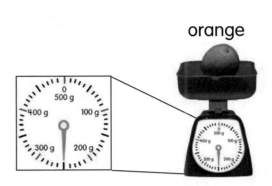

orange

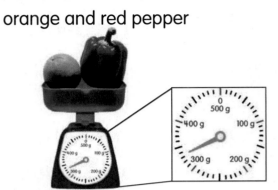

orange and red pepper

The mass of the orange is 250 grams.

330 − 250 = 80
The mass of the red pepper is 80 grams.
The orange is heavier than the red pepper.

250 − 80 = 170
The orange is 170 grams heavier than the red pepper.
The red pepper is 170 grams lighter than the orange.

## Guided Practice

**Look at the pictures.**
**Then answer each question.**

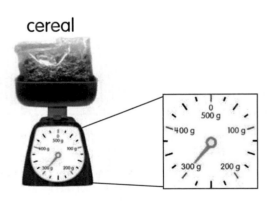

granola bars

cereal

**4** What is the mass of the granola bars?

**5** What is the mass of the cereal?

**6** Which is heavier?

How much heavier?

 # Hands-On Activity

 **STEP 1** Use a measuring scale and three objects, such as an apple, an orange, and a pear.

 **STEP 2** Place two of the objects on the scale. What is the mass of both objects?

 **STEP 3** Remove one object. What is the mass of the object left? What is the mass of the object you removed?

 **STEP 4** Place the three objects on the scale. What is the mass of all three objects? Find the mass of the third object.

# Let's Practice

**Look at the pictures.**
**Then answer the questions.**

1. The mass of the apple is [    ] grams.

2. The mass of the melon is [    ] grams.

3. The mass of the orange is [    ] grams.

4. The mass of the pineapple is [    ] grams.

5. The pineapple is [    ] grams heavier than the orange.

6. Order the fruits from lightest to heaviest.

   [    ] , [    ] , [    ] , [    ]

   lightest

# Look at the pictures.
# Then answer the questions.

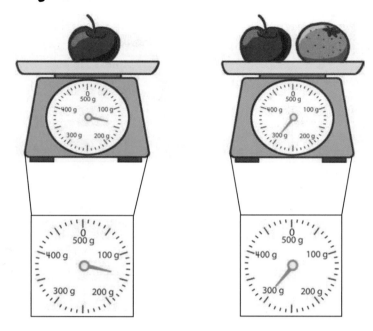

**7** What is the mass of the apple?

**8** What is the mass of the orange?

**9** Which is heavier?

**10** How much heavier?

**11** Which is lighter?

**12** How much lighter?

**Look at the pictures.**
**Then answer the questions.**

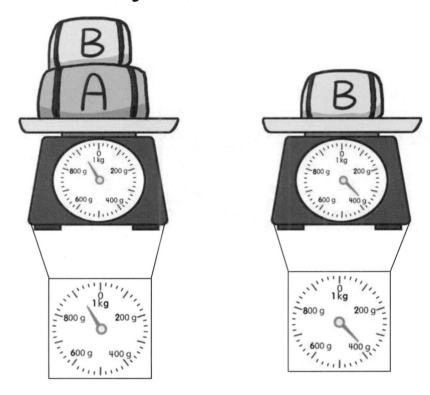

13) The mass of Package B is ▢ grams.

14) The mass of Package A is ▢ grams.

15) Package ▢ is ▢ grams
heavier than Package ▢.

16) Package ▢ is ▢ grams
lighter than Package ▢.

ON YOUR OWN

**Go to Workbook A:**
**Practice 4, pages 203–204**

# LESSON 5 Real-World Problems: Mass

## Lesson Objective

- Use bar models to solve problems about mass.

**Learn** **Use addition and subtraction to solve problems about mass.**

I can lift 2 kilograms.

I can lift 10 kilograms more than Ken!

I can only lift 9 kilograms.

2 kg

9 kg

Ken          Beth          Nathan

(a) What is the mass that Beth can lift?

(b) How much less mass can Ken lift than Nathan?

(a)

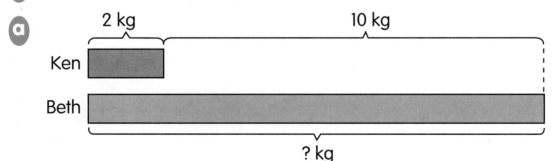

2 kg          10 kg

Ken

Beth

? kg

2 + 10 = 12
Beth can lift 12 kilograms.

(b)

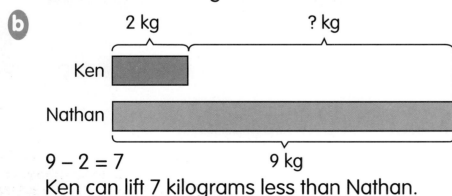

2 kg          ? kg

Ken

Nathan

9 – 2 = 7          9 kg
Ken can lift 7 kilograms less than Nathan.

# Guided Practice

**Solve.**
**Use the bar models to help you.**

**1** A grocer has 78 kilograms of potatoes.
He sells 12 kilograms of potatoes.
How many kilograms of potatoes does he have left?

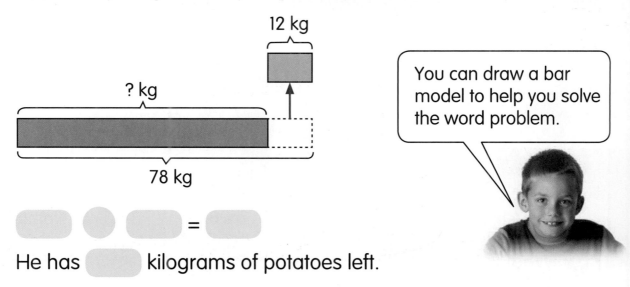

You can draw a bar model to help you solve the word problem.

He has ⬭ kilograms of potatoes left.

**2** The mass of the knight in armor is 80 kilograms.
The mass of the same knight without the armor is 61 kilograms.
What is the mass of the armor?

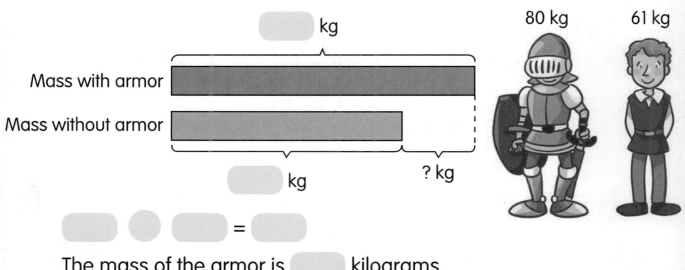

The mass of the armor is ⬭ kilograms.

 Hands-On Activity

**Choose a favorite book or object in the room each.**
**Record the masses of the objects on a chart like the one below.**

Example

| Name | Ali | Meiling | Raul | Cindy | Bianca |
|------|-----|---------|------|-------|--------|
| Mass of object | 2 kg | 3 kg | 10 kg | 3 kg | 1 kg |

Think of four questions you can ask using the masses.
Use your chart to answer the questions.

Example

1  How much heavier is Cindy's object than Bianca's?

2  What is the total mass of all objects that are
less than 3 kilograms?

3  How much lighter than Raul's object is Ali's object?

4  What is the total mass of both Ali's and Meiling's objects?

## Learn You can use bar models to solve real-world problems about mass.

The mass of a bag of flour is 950 grams.
Lin used 250 grams on Monday to bake a pizza.
She used 180 grams on Tuesday to bake some muffins.

**a** How much flour did Lin use altogether?

**b** How much flour was left at the end of the day?

**a**

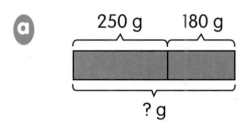

$250 + 180 = 430$

Lin used 430 grams of flour altogether.

**b**

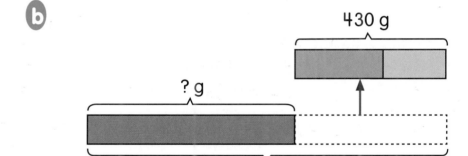

$950 - 430 = 520$

520 grams of flour was left at the end of the day.

# Guided Practice

**Solve.**
**Use the bar models to help you.**

**3** A chef has 88 kilograms of rice.
He uses 32 kilograms on Monday and 19 kilograms on Tuesday.
How much rice does the chef have left at the end of Tuesday?

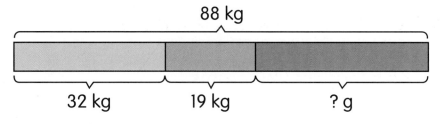

88 kg

32 kg     19 kg     ? g

⬭ ⬤ ⬭ = ⬭

The chef uses ⬭ kilograms of rice on Monday and Tuesday.

⬭ ⬤ ⬭ = ⬭

The chef has ⬭ kilograms of rice left at the end of Tuesday.

**4** The mass of a chicken is 2 kilograms.
A turkey is 5 kilograms heavier than the chicken.
What is the total mass of the chicken and the turkey?

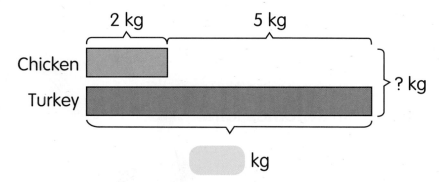

2 kg        5 kg

Chicken

Turkey        ? kg

⬭ kg

⬭ ⬤ ⬭ = ⬭

The mass of the turkey is ⬭ kilograms.

⬭ ⬤ ⬭ = ⬭

The total mass of the chicken and the turkey is ⬭ kilograms.

# Let's Practice

**Solve.**
**Use bar models to help you.**

**1** A box of cereal has a mass of 850 grams.
The mass of the cereal is 670 grams.
What is the mass of the empty box?

**2** A bag of onions has a mass of 240 grams.
A bag of carrots has a mass of 470 grams.
How much lighter is the bag of onions than the bag of carrots?

**3** A bag of peaches has a mass of 540 grams.
A bag of tomatoes has a mass of 150 grams.
How much heavier is the bag of peaches than
the bag of tomatoes?

**4** The mass of a chair is 10 kilograms.
A table is 22 kilograms heavier than the chair.
What is the total mass of the table and the chair?

**5** Sara has 630 grams of strawberries.
She eats 120 grams of strawberries.
She gives 350 grams of strawberries to Jose.
What is the mass of the strawberries left?

ON YOUR OWN

Go to Workbook A:
Practice 5, pages 205–208

## CRITICAL THINKING SKILLS
# Put On Your Thinking Cap!

**PROBLEM SOLVING**

**1** The picture shows some masses in a basket on a scale.

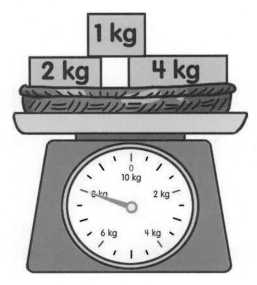

What is the mass of the basket?

**2**

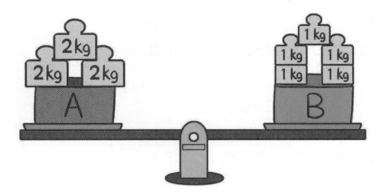

**a** Which is heavier, Box A or Box B?

**b** How much heavier?

**ON YOUR OWN**

Go to Workbook A:
Put on Your Thinking Cap!
pages 209–210

# Chapter Wrap Up

**You have learned...**

## Mass

### Measure

**1** In kilograms (kg)

The mass of the book is more than 1 kilogram.

The mass of the bottle is 2 kilograms.

**2** In grams (g)

The mass of the pita bread is 300 grams.

### Compare, add and subtract

**1** Compare and order

Box B is heavier than Box A.
Box B is lighter than Box C.
Box A is lightest.
Box C is heaviest.
The boxes are arranged in ord
from lightest to heaviest.

A , B , C

lightest

**BIG IDEA**

A scale can be used to measure and compare masses in kilograms and grams.

## Solve real-world problems

**2** Add to find mass

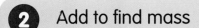

4 kg

4 + 3 = 7
The box has a mass of 7 kilograms.

**3** Subtract to find mass

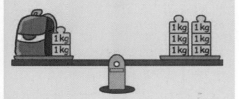

6 − 2 = 4
The bag has a mass of 4 kilograms.

**1** Mrs. Jones sends a letter with a mass of 50 grams.
She sends another letter with a mass of 60 grams.
What is the total mass of both letters?

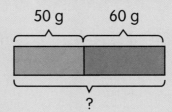

50 + 60 = 110
The total mass of both letters is 110 grams.

**2** A baker has 35 kilograms of flour.
He uses 16 kilograms to make biscuits.
How many kilograms of flour does he have left?

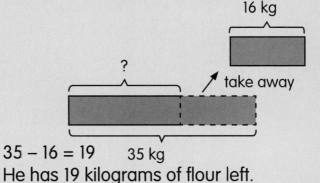

35 − 16 = 19     35 kg
He has 19 kilograms of flour left.

**ON YOUR OWN**

Go to Workbook A:
Chapter Review/Test,
pages 211–216

When I tap the glasses, there are two different sounds!

That's right! Different sounds are made when you tap containers that hold different volumes of water.

BIG IDEA

Volume is the amount of liquid in a container. Liters can be used to measure volume.

# Recall Prior Knowledge

## Measuring length and mass

### Length

1  stands for 1 unit.

The bracelet is about 5 units long.

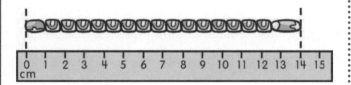

This ruler is smaller than in real life.

The bracelet is 14 centimeters long.

### Mass

1 ⚫ stands for 1 unit.

The mass of the pear is about 7 units.

The mass of the pear is 200 grams.

## Comparing length and weight

1 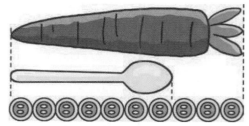 stands for 1 unit of length.

The carrot is 3 units longer than the spoon.

1 ⬭ stands for 1 unit of weight.

notebook

purse

peach

The notebook is as heavy as the purse.
The purse is 5 units lighter than the peach.

## Adding and subtracting without regrouping

56 + 23 = 79

```
   5 6
 + 2 3
 ─────
   7 9
```

78 − 45 = 33

```
   7 8
 − 4 5
 ─────
   3 3
```

## Adding and subtracting with regrouping

24 + 19 = 43

```
    1
   2 4
 + 1 9
 ─────
   4 3
```

51 − 37 = 14

```
    4
   5 ¹1
 − 3 7
 ─────
   1 4
```

**Find the missing number.**
**Then choose the correct answer.**

**1** 1 🖼 stands for 1 unit.

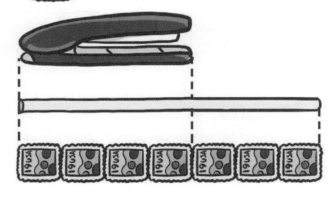

The straw is about ▢ units long.

The stapler is about 3 units (longer than / shorter than) the straw.

**2** 1 🍅 stands for 1 unit.

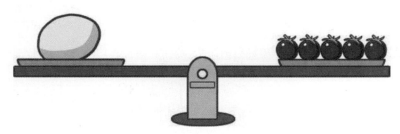

The mass of the egg is about ▢ units.

The egg is (heavier than / lighter than) one cherry tomato.

**Add or subtract.**

**3** 13 + 24 = ▢

**4** 67 − 35 = ▢

**5** 32 + 29 = ▢

**6** 56 − 28 = ▢

# LESSON 1 Getting to Know Volume

## Lesson Objective

• Explore and compare volume.

**Vocabulary**

| volume | more than | less than |
|---|---|---|
| as much as | most | least |

**Learn** You can use containers to hold water.

Let's fill these containers with water.

Now each container has an amount of colored water.

The amount of water is called the **volume** of water.

# Hands-On Activity

## Use three empty containers of different shapes.

Example

 **STEP 1** Fill one container with water. Mark the level of water on the container with a piece of tape.

 **STEP 2** Pour the water into another container.
Has the volume of water changed?
Pour the water back into the first container to check.

**STEP 3** Now pour the water into a third container. Has the volume of water changed? How can you check?

The volume of water remains the same even when it is poured into different containers.

### Learn **You can compare volumes.**

Bottles A and B are the same size.

Bottles A and B contain the same amount of water.

Bottle A          Bottle B

Bottle A contains **as much** water **as** Bottle B.

---

Bowls C, D and E are the same size.

Bowl C                    Bowl D                    Bowl E

The volume of water in Bowl C is **more than** the volume of water in Bowl D.

The volume of water in Bowl E is **less than** the volume of water in Bowl D.

Bowl C has the **most** water. Bowl E has the **least** amount of water.

## Guided Practice

**Fill in the blanks.**

Suzie pours juice into four bottles that are the same size.

Bottle A          Bottle B          Bottle C          Bottle D

**1** Did Suzie pour the same amount of juice into each bottle?

**2** Which bottle has the greatest amount of juice?

**3** Which bottle has the least amount of juice?

**4** Bottle [    ] has less juice than Bottle D.

**5** The volume of juice in Bottle D is less than the volume of juice in Bottle [    ] and in Bottle [    ].

**6** The volume of juice in Bottle A is more than the volume of juice in Bottle [    ] and in Bottle [    ].

**7** The volume of juice in Bottle A is less than the volume of juice in Bottle [    ].

# ✋ Hands-On Activity

Use five plastic glasses that are the same size.
Pour different amounts of liquid into each glass.
Put the glasses in order.
Begin with the glass with the least amount of liquid.
Draw your answer on a piece of paper.

## ⌒Learn  You can use containers to compare volumes.

All the juice from Container A and Container B is poured into glasses.
The glasses are the same size.

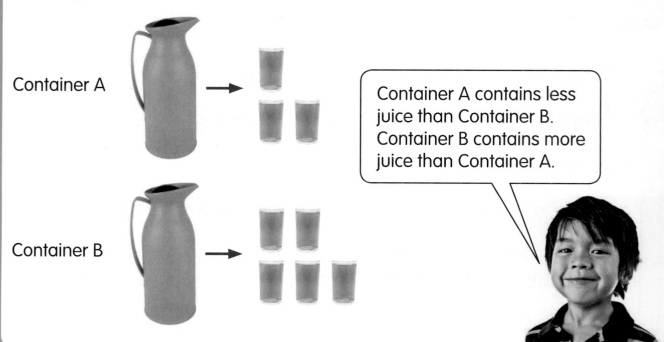

Container A

Container B

Container A contains less juice than Container B. Container B contains more juice than Container A.

# Guided Practice

## Find the missing letters or numbers.

Norman fills glasses of the same size with all the water from Container A, Container B, and Container C. The containers are the same size.

Container A

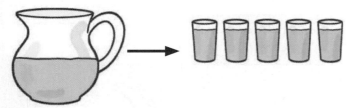

Container B

Container C

**8** Container ____ contains the least amount of water.

**9** Container ____ contains more water than Container A.

**10** Container C contains ____ more glasses of water than Container B.

**11** Container B contains ____ fewer glasses of water than Container A.

**12** Order Containers A, B, and C.
Begin with the container that has the greatest amount of water.

____ , ____ , ____
greatest

# Let's Practice

**Use the picture to answer each question.**

The picture shows four glasses, A, B, C, and D.
The glasses are the same size.

Glass A          Glass B          Glass C          Glass D

**1** In which glasses is the volume of juice the same?

**2** Which glass contains the greatest amount of juice?

**3** Which glass contains the least amount of juice?

**Look at the pictures.**
**Find the missing letters and words.**

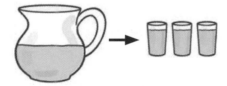

Container A        Container B                    Container C

**4** Container ____ contains ____ water than Container ____.

**5** Order Containers A, B, and C.
Begin with the container that has the least amount of water.

least ____ , ____ , ____

ON YOUR OWN

**Go to Workbook A:**
**Practice 1 and 2, pages 217–222**

# 2 Measuring in Liters

**Lesson Objective**

• Use liters to estimate, measure, and compare volume.

**Learn** **You can tell if a container can hold more or less than a liter.**

This carton contains
1 liter of milk.

This glass contains less than
1 liter of milk.

You use liters (L) to measure
the volume of liquid.

The **liter** is a unit of volume.
**L** stands for liter.
Read 1 L as 1 liter.
A liter is used to measure
greater volume.

These are some containers that hold less than 1 liter of liquid each.

Name other objects that hold less than 1 liter of liquid.

Continued on next page

These are some containers that hold more than 1 liter of liquid.

Name other containers that hold more than 1 liter of liquid.

This is a 1-liter **measuring cup**. It contains 1 liter of water.

This measuring cup contains less than 1 liter of water.

This measuring cup contains more than 1 liter of water.

## Guided Practice

**Use more than or less than to complete each sentence.**

1
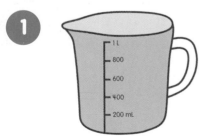

This measuring cup contains ⬜ 1 liter of water.

2

This measuring cup contains ⬜ 1 liter of water.

### Learn

## You can use a measuring cup to measure volume.

This container holds some milk.
Is the amount of milk more or less than 1 liter?
How can you check?

> I can pour the milk into a 1-liter measuring cup to check the volume of milk.

## Guided Practice

**Look at the pictures.
Then find the missing numbers and letters.**

**3**    Container A contains ▭ liters of water.

**4**    Container B contains ▭ liters of water.

**5**    Container ▭ contains more water than Container ▭ .

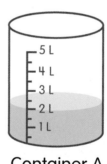 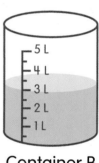

Container A    Container B

**Look at the pictures.
Then find the missing numbers.**

**6**    Container A

**7**    Container B

Container A has ▭ liters of water.

Container B has ▭ liters of water.

# Let's Practice

**Fill in the blanks.**

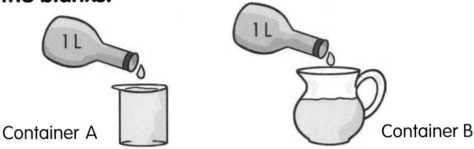

Container A          Container B

1  Container [      ] can hold about 1 liter of water.

2  Container [      ] can hold more than 1 liter of water.

**Name the containers that hold less than 1 liter.**

3

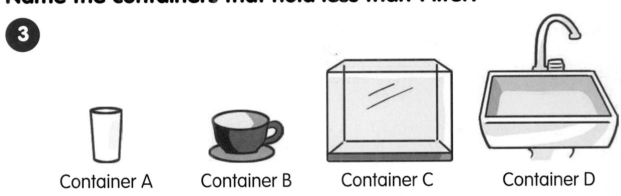

Container A      Container B      Container C      Container D

**Look at the pictures.**
**Then fill in the blanks.**

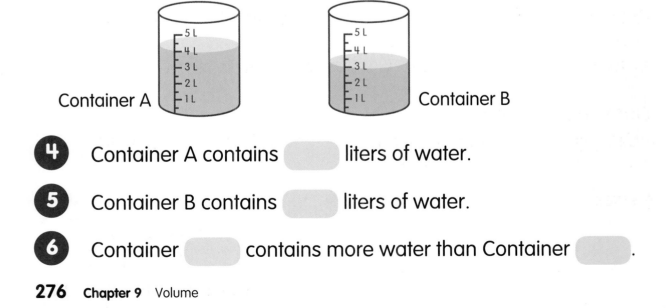

Container A                    Container B

4  Container A contains [      ] liters of water.

5  Container B contains [      ] liters of water.

6  Container [      ] contains more water than Container [      ].

**Look at the pictures.**
**Then find the missing numbers and letters.**

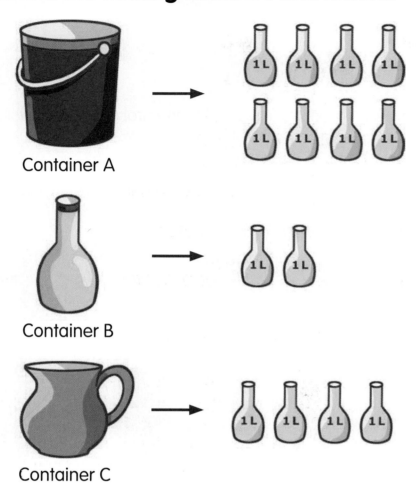

Container A

Container B

Container C

**7** Container A has [    ] liters of water.

**8** Container [    ] has the least amount of water.

**9** Container B has [    ] liters of water less than Container C.

**10** Container A contains twice as much water as Container [    ].

**11** Order the containers.
Begin with the container that has the greatest amount of water.

[    ] [    ], [    ]

greatest

ON YOUR OWN

Go to Workbook A:
Practice 3, pages 223–226

# Real-World Problems: Volume

## Lesson Objective

- Use bar models, addition, and subtraction to solve real-world problems about volume.

**Learn** **You can use bar models to help you add and subtract volume.**

Jack has two bottles of orange juice.
During the week, he drinks all the orange juice.
How much orange juice does he drink in all?

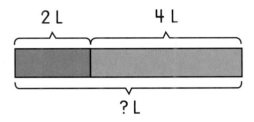

2 L        4L

$2 + 4 = 6$

He drinks 6 liters of orange juice in all.

. . . . . . . . . . . . . . . . . . . . . . . . . . . . . . . . . . . . . . . . . . . . . . . . . . . . . . . . . . . .

There are 17 liters of water in a pail.
8 liters of the water spill.
How much water is left?

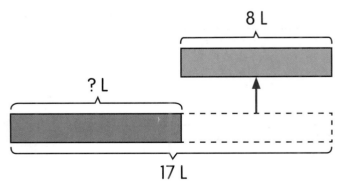

$17 - 8 = 9$

9 liters of water are left.

# Guided Practice

**Solve.**
**Use the bar models to help you.**

**1** A tank has 34 liters of water.
George pours 17 more liters of water into the tank.
How much water does the tank have now?

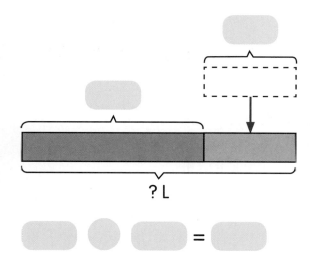

? L

[ ] ⬤ [ ] = [ ]

The tank has [ ] liters of water now.

**2** On Saturday, the Stevens family uses 32 liters of water.
The Martin family uses 28 liters of water on the same day.
How much more water does the Stevens family use than
the Martin family?

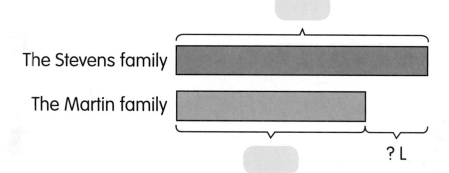

The Stevens family

The Martin family

? L

[ ] ⬤ [ ] = [ ]

The Stevens family uses [ ] liters more water than the Martin family.

**3** The Dairy Store has 98 liters of milk.
In the morning, 15 liters are sold.
In the afternoon, another 42 liters are sold.
How many liters of milk are left?

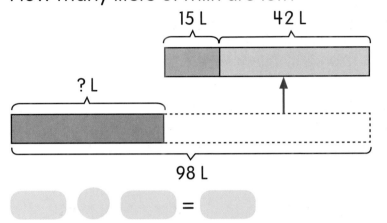

15 L       42 L

? L

98 L

☐ ◯ ☐ = ☐

The Dairy Store sold ☐ liters of milk in all.

☐ ◯ ☐ = ☐

There are ☐ liters of milk left.

First, find the volume of milk sold.

**4** Factory A uses 64 liters of oil in a week.
Factory B uses 29 liters of oil less than Factory A.
How many liters of oil do they use in all?

64 L

Factory A

Factory B

? L

L       29 L

☐ ◯ ☐ = ☐

Factory B uses ☐ liters of oil.

☐ ◯ ☐ = ☐

First, find the volume of oil Factory B uses.

Factory A and Factory B use ☐ liters of oil in all.

## Let's Practice

**Solve.**

**1**  There are 55 liters of orange juice for a party.
After the party, 18 liters of orange juice are left.
How many liters of orange juice were served?

**2**  A medium tank can hold 76 liters of water.
It can hold 12 liters of water less than a large tank.
How many liters of water can a large tank hold?

**3**  Factory A uses 45 liters of oil in a week.
Factory B uses 29 more liters of oil in a week than Factory A.
How many liters of oil do both factories use altogether?

**4**  Pail A contains 15 liters of water.
It contains 3 liters more water than Pail B.
Betsy pours another 4 liters of water into Pail B.
What is the volume of water in Pail B now?

**ON YOUR OWN**

Go to Workbook A:
Practice 4, pages 227–230

## CRITICAL THINKING SKILLS
## Put On Your Thinking Cap!

**PROBLEM SOLVING**

Tank X has 8 liters of water in it.
Tank Y is the same size.
It has 6 liters of water in it.
Jason pours more water into Tank Y until it has
1 more liter of water than Tank X.
How many liters of water did he pour into Tank Y?

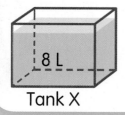
Tank X

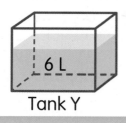
Tank Y

**ON YOUR OWN**

Go to Workbook A:
Put on Your Thinking Cap!
pages 231–232

# Chapter Wrap Up

**You have learned...**

## Volume

### Understand volume

1 Volume is the amount of liquid in a container.

2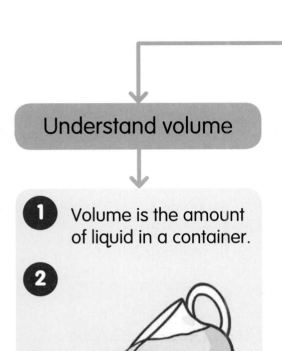

Volume remains the same when a liquid is poured into different containers.

### Compare

1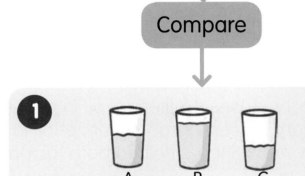

A    B    C

The volume of water in Glass A is more than the volume of water in Glass C.

Order the glasses.
Begin with the glass that holds the least amount of water: Glass C, Glass A, Glass B.

2

Container X contains 2 glasses of water.
Container Y contains 4 glasses of water.
Container X contains 2 fewer glasses of water than Container Y.
Container Y contains 2 more glasses of water than Container X.

BIG IDEA

Volume is the amount of liquid in a container. Liters can be used to measure volume.

## Measure

**1** Liter is the unit used to measure volume. L stands for liter.

There is 1 liter of water in the container.

**2**

There are 4 liters of water in the container.

## Solve real-world problems

Linda has 7 liters of juice.
She buys another 5 liters of juice.
Rodney has 4 liters of juice less than Linda.
How many liters of juice does Rodney have?

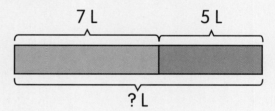

$7 + 5 = 12$
Linda has 12 liters of juice.

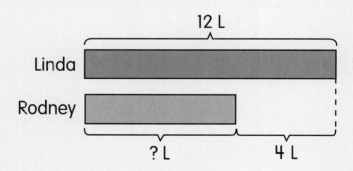

$12 - 4 = 8$
Rodney has 8 liters of juice.

ON YOUR OWN

Go to Workbook A:
Chapter Review/Test,
pages 233–236

Blank

 **Focus Lessons**

## Chapter 5

# Odd and Even Numbers

COMMON CORE

**2.OA.3.** Determine whether a group of objects (up to 20) has an odd or even number of members. Write an equation to express an even number as a sum of two equal addends.

## Lesson Objectives

- Make groups of 2 to find odd and even numbers.
- Understand that an even number is the sum of two equal numbers.

**Vocabulary**
odd number
even number

Learn

### You can find odd and even numbers by making groups of 2.

Put 5 apples into groups of 2.

There is 1 apple left.

5 is an **odd number**.

Put 6 pears into groups of 2.

There are no pears left.

6 is an **even number**.

# Let's Practice

**Circle groups of 2.**
**Write the number.**
**Then write *odd* or *even***

**1**

There is _____  left.

7 is an _____ number.

**2**

There are _____ ▪ left.

10 is an _____ number.

## Solve.

**3** Is 17 an odd or even number?
Draw circles, then circle groups of 2.

17 is an _____ number.

**An even number has two parts that are the same.**

4 is an even number.

4    =    2    +    2

10 is an even number.

When you add two numbers that are the same, you will always get an even number.

10    =    5    +    5

# Let's Practice

**Complete.**

**1**   $6 = 3 +$ _____

**2**   $18 =$ _____ $+ 9$

**3**   _____ $= 8 + 8$

**4**   If you add 4 and 3, will the answer be an even or odd number?

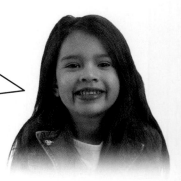

The parts must be the same.

# Glossary

## A

- **add**

  Put together two or
  more parts to make a whole.

  $$5 + 3 = 8$$

  part  part  whole

- **as heavy as**

  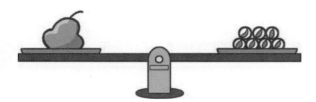

  The pear is as heavy as 7 marbles.

- **as much as**

  Container A      Container B

  Container A has 4 liters of water.
  Container B has 4 liters of water.

  Container A contains as much
  water as Container B.

## B

- **bar models**

  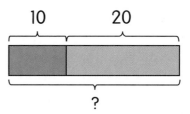

  This is an example of
  a bar model.
  Use bar models to help you add
  and subtract.

# C

- **centimeter (cm)**

  Centimeter is a metric unit of length.
  Write cm for centimeter.

  The crayon is 8 centimeters long.

- **compare**

  When you compare, you find out which set has more or fewer things.

  Compare the number of pears and strawberries.

  There are 2 more pears than strawberries.
  There are 2 fewer strawberries than pears.

# D

- **divide**

  Put into equal groups or share equally.

  $$15 \div 3 = 5$$

  Divide 15 dog biscuits into 3 equal groups of 5 dog biscuits.

- **division sentence**

  $6 \div 2 = 3$ is a division sentence.

- **dot paper**

  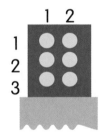

  This is dot paper.
  It shows 3 rows of 2.

# E

- **equal**

  Having the same amount or number.

  3 is the same as 2 + 1.

  $3 = 2 + 1$

  equal sign

- **equal groups**

  Having the same amount in each group.
  You add equal groups to multiply.
  You subtract equal groups to divide.

  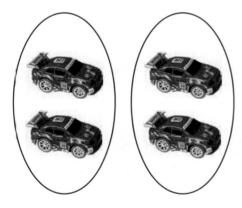

  $2 \times 2 = 4$

  $4 \div 2 = 2$

  There are 2 toy cars in each group.

- **expanded form**

  $400 + 30 + 2$ is the expanded form of 432.

# F

- **fact family**

  $2 + 4 = 6 \qquad 4 + 2 = 6$
  $6 - 2 = 4 \qquad 6 - 4 = 2$

  This is a fact family.

# G

- **gram**

  Gram is a metric unit of mass. Write g for gram.

  The grapes have a mass of 880 grams.

- **greater than (>)**

 >

5 > 4

5 is greater than 4.

- **greatest**

20 is the greatest number.

- **group**
  See **equal groups**.

**H**————————

- **heavier than**

The hen is heavier than the chick.

- **heaviest**

The bag of rice is the heaviest.

- **height**

The height of the fence is 2 meters.

- **hundred**

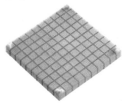

10 tens = 100

- **hundreds**

| Hundreds | Tens | Ones |
|----------|------|------|
|  | | |
| 2 | 5 | 8 |

258 = 2 hundreds 5 tens 8 ones

# J

- **join**

  When you join sets, you add the number of objects in one set to the number of objects in another set to find the total.

  I have 4 apples.

  I have 3 apples.

  4 + 3 = 7
  They have 7 apples in all.

  See **add**.

# K

- **kilogram**

  Kilogram is a metric unit of mass. Write kg for kilogram.

  The mass of the bag of oranges is 5 kilograms.

# L

- **least**

  2 is the least number.

- **length**

  Describes how long something is.

  A ——————————————— B

  To find the length of the drawing, measure from Point *A* to Point *B*.

  See **meter** and **centimeter.**

- **less than (<)**

  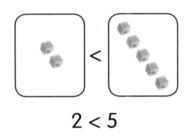

  2 < 5

  2 is less than 5.

- **lighter than**

  The hen is lighter than the cat.

- **lightest**

  The bag of sugar is the lightest.

- **liter**

  Liter is a metric unit of volume.
  Write L for liter.

  This carton contains 1 liter of milk.

- **longer**

  Longer

- **longest**

Longest

**M**

- **mass**

  How heavy an object or a set of objects is.

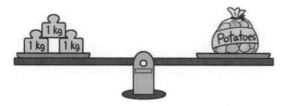

  The mass of the potatoes is 3 kilograms.

  See **kilogram** and **gram**.

- **measuring cup**

  This is a 1-liter measuring cup. It contains 1 liter of water.

- **measuring scale**

  This tool measures the mass of an object.

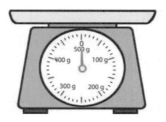

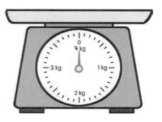

- **meter (m)**

  Meter is a metric unit of length. Write m for meter.

  The car is 3 meters long.

- **meterstick**

A meterstick is used to measure length.

- **more than**

There are more ⭐ than ♥.

There is 1 more ⭐ than ♥.

- **most**

Joe    Luis    Pepe

Pepe has the most marbles.

- **multiplication sentence**

$3 \times 3 = 9$ is a multiplication sentence.

- **multiplication story**

There are 2 children.
Each child has 3 oranges.

$2 \times 3 = 6$
They have 6 oranges in all.

- **multiply**
Put all the equal groups together.

There are 5 groups.
There are 2 muffins in each group.

$5 \times 2 = 10$
There are 10 muffins in all.

## place-value chart

| Hundreds | Tens | Ones |
|----------|------|------|
|          |      |      |

# R

## regroup

Sometimes you need to regroup numbers when adding and subtracting.

When you regroup numbers, you change:

- 10 ones to 1 ten or 1 ten to 10 ones
- 10 tens to 1 hundred or 1 hundred to 10 tens

**Example**

$$\begin{array}{r} \overset{1}{4}\,5 \\ +\ 3\,8 \\ \hline 8\,3 \end{array} \qquad \begin{array}{r} \overset{5}{\cancel{6}}\,{}^{1}5 \\ -\ 2\,7 \\ \hline 3\,8 \end{array}$$

## related addition and subtraction facts

See **fact family**.

## related multiplication facts

$5 \times 2 = 10$

$2 \times 5 = 10$

These are related multiplication facts.

## related multiplication and division facts

$5 \times 2 = 10$

$10 \div 5 = 2$

$2 \times 5 = 10$

$10 \div 2 = 5$

These are related multiplication and division facts.

## repeated addition

You can use repeated addition to find the number of turtles.

3 + 3 + 3 + 3 = 12
Groups of 3 are added 4 times.

See **equal groups**.

## repeated subtraction

You can use repeated subtraction to find the number of groups.

6 − 2 − 2 − 2 = 0
Groups of 2 are subtracted 3 times.

See **equal groups**.

# S

## set

A collection of items.

There are 2 sets of toy airplanes.

## share

Divide into equal groups.

## shorter

shorter

- **shortest**

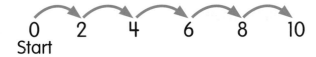 shortest

- **skip-count**

Skip-counting by 2s:

0  2  4  6  8  10
Start

Skip-counting by 5s:

0  5  10  15  20  25
Start

Skip-counting by 10s:

0  10  20  30  40  50
Start

- **standard form**

657 is the standard form of 657.

- **subtract**

Take away one part from the whole to find the other part.

$$5 - 2 = 3$$
whole  part  part

T _____

- **take away**

See **subtract**.

- **taller**

taller

- **tallest**

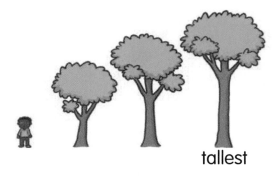

tallest

- **times**

See **multiply**.

- **thousand**

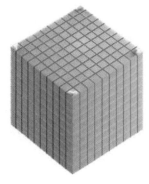

10 hundreds = 1,000

- **unit**

Units are used to measure objects.

 can be used to measure. It represents 1 unit.

The bracelet is about 5 units long.

**V**

- **volume**

The amount of liquid a container has.

See **liter**.

# W

- **width**

  How wide an object is.

  The width of the pencil case is 10 centimeters.

- **word form**

  Three hundred twenty-eight is the word form of 328.

# Index

**Bar models, 96**
    length, 216–220; *122–126, 206–208, 218;*
        *WB 179–182; WB 89–90, 96, 169–171*
    mass, 253–258; *209–211, 215–216, 218;*
        *WB 213–214; WB 172–173, 181*
    numbers,
        comparing sets, *See* Set–compare
        joining sets, *See* Set–join
        part-part-whole, *See* Part-part-whole
        taking away sets, *See* Set–take away
    volume, 278–281, 283

Base-ten blocks, *See* Manipulatives

Communication
    Math Journal, 65, 70, 107, 132, 169, 175, 206; *16,*
        *27, 38, 146, 200, 204; WB 18,*
        *91–92, 118, 149–150, 207–208, 228*

**Comparing, 18**
    fewest, **231**
    greater than, **18,** 19–23, 33; *72, 83, 85; WB 13–14,*
        *23, 99*
    greatest, 24, 25–26, 30, 33; *63, 65, 84–89, 99;*
        *WB 23, 43–44, 67, 245; WB 36*
    height, *See* Length
    least, 24, 25–26, 30, 33; *63, 65, 84–89, 99;*
        *WB 23, 43, 67, 245; WB 36, 38*
    length, *See* Length
    less than, **19,** 26–28, 31, 33, *192–195; WB 13–14,*
        *99, 165–166, 168; WB 24–25, 35, 63–66*
    mass, *See* Mass
    more than, 26, 27–28, 31, *192–195; 52, 62–63, 67,*
        *85, 97–98; WB 165–166, 168, 25, 35, 63–66*
    most, *WB 24*
    numbers, *See* Place value
    using inequalities, 18–23, 33, 99
    sets, *See* Sets
    width, *See* Length
    volume, *See* Volume

Connecting cubes, *See* Manipulatives

Counters, See Manipulatives

Counting, **6,**
    on by 1s, 10s, and 100s to 1,000, 6–10; *WB 1–6,*
        *16–18, 20, 24, 99*
    counting back, 27–28, 31–33; *WB 16–17, 20,*
        *23, 99*
    counting on, 6–10, 26–30, 31, 33; *WB 1–6,*
        *16–20, 24, 99*
    skip-counting, *See* Multiplication

Cube, *See* Geometry

Cumulative Review, *See* Assessment

Difference, *See* Subtraction
    estimate, 35, 37–38, 41; *WB 19–20*

Division, **134**
    basic facts, 134–141; *WB 111–114*
    equal groups, **134,** 135, 140–141, 148; *WB 111,*
        *121*
    inverse operation, *See* Inverse operation
    repeated subtraction, 136, 137–139, 141, 146; *WB*
        *112–114, 117, 121–122, 158*
    related division facts, *179; 184–189, 193;*
    sentence, 134, 135, 137–141, 143–144, 146;
        *184–188, 192–193, 201–204, 206, 209, 213,*
        *218–219; WB 111–114, 117–118, 121–122,*
        *124, 145–148, 152, 155–156, 158–159, 161,*
        *163–164; WB 151–154, 166–168, 170–175*
    sharing equally, **134,** 135, 140–141; *201–202,*
        *207–208, 219; WB 111; WB 165–168*
    using related multiplication facts, 179–185, 188;
        *WB 145–148*

Dot grid paper, *See* Shapes and Patterns
Dot paper, *See* Manipulatives

Pages listed in regular type refer to Student Book A.
Pages in blue type refer to Student Book B.
Pages listed in *italic* type refer to Workbook (WB) A.
Pages in *blue italic type* refer to Workbook (WB) B.
Pages in **boldface** type show where a term
is introduced.

Join, *See* Set-join

Length, **192**
  about, **114,** 116; *WB 70*
  comparing,
    longer, **197,** 198–199, 211–215; 107–108,
      110, 117–121; *WB 166, 169, 172,*
      *188, 235; WB 67–68, 75–76, 81, 83, 85*
    longest, **197,** 200, 211, 214; 107; *WB, 68, 73*
    shorter, **197,** 198–200, 211–213; 107–109,
      117–118, 120, 128; *WB 166, 170, 172;*
      *WB 75–76, 79, 81, 83*
    shortest, **197,** 200, 211; 107, 118; *WB 170,*
      *188; WB 85*
    taller, **196,** 200, 110, 128; *WB 169–170; WB 67*
    tallest, **196,** 200; 110; *WB 170*
    estimating, 194, 204; *WB 168, 187*
    height, **193,** 194, 196, 207, 215; 104, 106;
      *WB 73, 165, 167, 169–170, 185; WB 63*
  tools,
    centimeter ruler, **201;** *WB 171–178, 188*
    inch ruler, **113,** 115–117, 119–120; *WB 79–82*
    meterstick, **192,** 193–200; *WB 165–170, 185*
  units,
    centimeters (cm), **201,** 202–215, 218–220,
      222–223; *WB 171–178, 180–183, 185, 188,*
      *190, 235–236, 246, 248*
    feet (ft), **100,** 103–110, 122–123, 126–129; *WB 73–78*
    inches (in.), **100,** 111–121, 124–125, 126, 128–129;
      *WB 79–86*
    meters (m), **192,** 193–200, 216–217, 220–221,
      221–223; *WB 165–170, 179–180, 185–186, 189*
  width, **193,** 194, 206; *WB 167, 169–170, 186*

Let's Explore, *See* Exploration

Let's Practice, *See* Practice

Lines,
  part of a line, **115,** 115–117, 120, 253–257, 266;
    *WB 209–244*
  curve, 113, 253–257, 266; *WB 209–244*

Manipulatives,
  balance scale, 231–235, 237, 240, 243, 260–261;
    *WB 191, 194, 196–197, 207, 209*
  base-ten blocks, 6–12, 17–21, 23, 33, 38–40, 42,
    44, 46–47, 49–50, 61–63, 67–68, 72–74, 76,
    78–80, 84–85; *WB 1, 4–5, 7–9, 21–22, 245–246*
  cards, 9
  centimeter ruler, 201–215, 218–220, 222–223; *WB*
    *171–178*
  classroom objects,
    counters, 139
    craftsticks, 139
    string, 105, 113, 116; *WB 167–168, 172–173; WB 66, 69*
  computer, *See* Technology
  connecting cubes, 92, 96–99; 8
  dot paper, 156–160, 168, 171, 176–178, 187–188;
    161–162, 164, 170–173, 179–182, 191–192;
    *WB 129–132, 137–140, 153–156, 160–161;*
    *WB 135–138, 143–146, 154*
  foot ruler, 103–108; *WB 73–78*
  inch ruler, 111–121; *WB 79–88*
  measuring cup, 274–276, 283; *WB 221–224, 229,*
    *232–233, 239, 248*
  measuring scale, 229–234, 236–238, 241,
    243–245, 248, 250–252, 260; *WB 191–196,*
    *198–203, 208–212, 248*

  meterstick, 192–200; *WB 165–170, 185*
  number cube, 9

Mass, **228**
  comparing,
    as heavy as, **229;** *WB 191, 208*
    heavier than, **235,** 246, 248, 252, 260; *WB*
      *203–204, 211*
    heaviest, **237,** 239, 245, 247, 260; *WB 191,*
      *203–204, 208, 212*
    less than, **229;** *WB 191*
    lighter than, **235,** 240, 246, 248, 252, 260; *WB*
      *203–204, 208*
    lightest, **237,** 239, 245, 247, 260; *WB 191,*
      *203–204, 211–212*
    more than, **230;** *WB 191,*

Pages listed in regular type refer to Student Book A.
Pages in blue type refer to Student Book B.
Pages listed in *italic* type refer to Workbook (WB) A.
Pages in *blue italic type* refer to Workbook (WB) B.
Pages in **boldface** type show where a term
is introduced.

estimating, 230, 247
ordering, 237, 239, 245, 250, 260; *WB 194, 204, 207, 212*
tools,
> balance scale, 231–235, 237, 240, 243, 260–261; *WB 191, 194, 196–197, 207, 209*
> measuring scale, **229,** 230–234, 236–238, 241, 243–245, 248, 250–252, 260; *WB 191–196, 198–203, 208–212, 248*

units,
> gram (g), **240,** 241–252, 260; *WB 197–206, 208–211, 236–237, 246, 248; WB 169*
> kilogram (kg), **228,** 229–239, 260; *WB 191–196, 205–206, 209, 211, 236–237; WB 168–170*

Math Journal, *See* Communication

Measurement, *See* Length, Mass, *and* Volume

Metric system, *See* Length, Mass, *and* Volume

Mid-Year Review, *See* Assessment

Money
bills,
> one dollar, 46–51, 53, 56–57, 61, 64, 71; *WB 23–26, 28, 30–33, 37–38, 43*
> five dollar, 46–49, 53–57, 61, 64, 71; *WB 23, 26, 28, 30–31, 33, 37–38*
> ten dollar, 46–49, 53, 55–57, 61, 64, 71; *WB 23, 25–26, 28, 31, 37*
> twenty dollar, 46–49, 56–57, 71; *WB 23, 28, 37, 43*

coins,
> dime, 43–45, 50–57, 61, 64; *WB 24–26, 28–29, 31–33, 38, 43*
> nickel, 43–45, 52, 55–57, 61, 71; *WB 24, 29–33, 38, 43*
> penny, 43–45, 52, 57, 71; *WB 24, 29, 30, 43*
> quarter, 43–45, 50–57, 61, 64, 71; *WB 24–26, 28–32, 38, 43*

Multiplication, **127**
> basic facts, 127–133; *WB 107–110, 246*
> commutative property, 160–161, 171–172, 176–178, 187; *WB 132, 139–140, 144, 160–161, 248*
> dot paper, **156,** 157–161, 168–169, 171–172, 176–178, 187; *161–162, 164, 170–173, 179–182, 191–192; WB 129–132, 137–140, 153–156, 160–161; WB 139–142, 147–150, 158*
> equal groups, 127, 128–131, 148; *WB 121*

inverse operations, *See* Inverse operations
related multiplication facts, **160,** 161, 179–185; *184–189, 193 WB 145–148, 153, 160–161; 51–154, 158*
repeated addition, **127,** 128–129, 148; *WB 108–110, 115, 121–122, 157*
skip-counting, **153**
> by 2s, 153–155, 186–187; *WB 127–128, 156, 160*
> by 3s, 166–169, 191; *WB 133–134, 153*
> by 4s, 175–176, 178; *WB 141–142, 153*
> by 5s, 162–167, 187; *WB 133–135, 153, 156, 160*
> by 10s, 174–175, 187; *WB 141–143, 160*

sentence, **127,** 128–132, 142, 145, 148, 153–161, 164–165, 167–172, 174–182, 184, 186–188; *166–176, 178–183, 187–189, 191–193, 198, 206–211, 213–216, 218–219, 225–226, 238–239, 247; WB 107–110, 115, 118, 121–123, 128–144, 145–156, 157, 159–163; WB 133–139, 141–147, 153–154, 155–160, 165, 168–170, 172, 177–178, 199–200*

stories, **130,** 133; *WB 109–110, 115 , 121, 135–138, 149–150, 156, 162–164*

table
> of 2, 160, 187
> of 3, 172, 191
> of 4, 182, 191
> of 5, 171, 187; *WB 149–150*
> of 10, 176, 187; *WB 149–150*

times, **127,** 128–133, 142, 145, 147, 148; *WB 107–110, 115–116, 118, 121–123, 125, 127–157, 159–163*

Number cube, *See* Manipulatives

Numbers, **6**
> 101 through 1,000, 6–10
> comparing, *See* Comparing
> ordering, **24,** 25–26, 30, 33; *WB 15–16, 23, 43, 67, 100, 247*
> patterns, *See* Patterns
> place value, *See* Place value
> reading, *See* Place value
> writing, *See* Place Value

difference, *WB 7–10*
fact family, 57
inverse operations, *See* Inverse operations
mental, *WB 11–14*
models for,
  abstract, 98–99, 101–102, 106–108,
    111–115, 117–123, 216–220, 278–281,
    283; *WB 75–76, 79–85, 87, 89–92,*
    *94–98, 101–103, 105, 112–114, 117,*
    *180–181, 189–190, 205–206, 212–214,*
    *225–227, 240–242, 249, 252; WB 7–10*
  concrete, 61–63, 67–68, 72–74, 78–80,
    84–85
  pictorial, 98–99, 101–102, 106–108,
    111–115, 117–123, 216–220, 254,
    256–258, 278–281, 283; *WB 75–76,*
    *79–85, 87, 89–92, 94–98, 102–103, 105,*
    *205–206, 213–214, 225–227, 240–242,*
    *249*
hundreds from a 3-digit number; *WB 7–9, 14*
ones from a 2-digit number; *WB 11*
ones from a 3-digit number; *WB 12*
tens from a 3-digit number; *WB 7–9, 13*
place value, *See* place value
real-world problems, *See* Real-world problems
regrouping,
  hundreds as tens, 72–77, 79, 81–83;
    *WB 57–60, 67, 69–72, 101–102, 245, 247*
  hundreds, tens, and ones, 78–83; *WB 61–64,*
    *67, 69–72, 101–102, 247*
  tens as ones, 67–71, 78, 81–83; *WB 53–56,*
    *67, 69–72, 101–102, 244-245, 247*
  repeated, *See* Division
strategies,
  comparing sets, *See* Set–compare
  part-part-whole, *See* Part-part-whole
  subtract 100 then add the extra tens, 24
  subtract the hundreds, 25
  subtract the ones, 21
  subtract 10 then add the extra ones, 20, 22
  subtract the tens, 23
  taking away sets, *See* Set–take away
without regrouping up to 3-digit numbers,
    61–66;
    *WB 49–52, 67*
with zeros, 57

Sum, *See* Addition
  estimate, 34, 37–38; *WB 15, 19–20, 22*

Surfaces
  flat, 258–264, 266; *WB 215*
  curved, 258–264, 266; *WB 215*

Taking away, *See* Set–take away

Tally chart, *See* Picture Graphs

Technology
  Computers, 278

Tens, *See* Place value
Thousand, *See* Place value

Time,
  A.M. 142–149 ; *WB 107–110, 121*
  elapsed, 150–153, 155; *WB 111–117*
  hour hand, *WB 104–106, 111*
  minute hand, 133–136; *WB 97–100, 103, 105, 111*
  ordering, 145, 149; *WB 110*
  P.M., 142–149; *WB 107–110, 121*
  reading, 137–141; *WB 101–102, 106*
  writing, 137–141; *WB 101–102, 106, 115, 121*

Tools (of measure), See Length, Mass, and Volume

Triangle, See Geometry

Units (of measure), *See* Length, Mass, *and* Volume

Vocabulary, 6, 11, 18, 38, 42, 61, 103, 109, 127, 134, 153,
    156, 192, 196, 201, 228, 235, 240, 266, 273; *WB 21,*
    *45, 69, 95, 121, 153, 185–186, 211, 231*

Volume, **266**
  comparing,
    as much as, 268; *WB 215*
    least, 268, 269, 271–272, 277; *WB 216–220, 231*
    less than, 268, 269, 272, 273–274, 277; *WB*
    *215, 231, 248*

Pages listed in regular type refer to Student Book A.
Pages in blue type refer to Student Book B.
Pages listed in *italic* type refer to Workbook (WB) A.
Pages in *blue italic type* refer to Workbook (WB) B.
Pages in **boldface** type show where a term
is introduced.

more than, 268, 269, 271–272, 274, 276; *WB 215, 217, 231, 248*

most, 268, 272; *WB 216–220, 238*

ordering, 270–272; *WB 219, 224*

tool,

measuring cup, **274,** 275–276, 283; *WB 221–224, 229, 232–233, 238, 248*

units,

liters (L), **273,** 274–283; *WB 221–234, 238–240, 242, 248; WB 170–171, 178*

Width, *See* Length

Word form, *See* Place Value

Zero,

addition with, *See* Addition

in place value, *See* Place value

subtracting across, *See* Subtraction

subtraction with, *See* Subtraction

# Photo Credits

Blank